**COMING
SOON**

DANIA SCHIFTAN

TRANSLATED BY **ANNE POSTEN**
ILLUSTRATIONS BY **NICOLE KIM**

COMING SOON

Great Orgasms and Better Sex at Your Fingertips

GREYSTONE BOOKS
VANCOUVER/BERKELEY

First published in English by Greystone Books in 2021
Originally published in German as *Coming Soon: Orgasmus ist Übungssache*, copyright
© 2018 by Piper Verlag GmbH, München/Berlin
English translation copyright © 2021 by Anne Posten
Illustrations copyright © 2021 by Nicole Kim

21 22 23 24 25 5 4 3 2 1

Greystone Books Ltd.
greystonebooks.com

Cataloguing data available from Library and Archives Canada
ISBN 978-1-77164-558-4 (pbk.)
ISBN 978-1-77164-559-1 (epub)

Copy editing by Paula Ayer
Proofreading by Alison Strobel
Indexing by Alison Jacques
Cover and text design by Belle Wuthrich
Cover art © by Lynne Rutherford

Printed and bound in Canada on ancient-forest-friendly paper by Friesens

This work reflects the ideas and opinions of the author. It aims to provide useful
information on the topics covered in these pages. Neither the author nor the publisher is
offering medical, health, or other professional services in this book. Before putting the
suggestions in this book into practice or drawing conclusions from them, readers should
consult their general practitioner or another competent health professional. The author
and the publisher are not responsible for any liability, damage, loss, or risk, whether
personal or otherwise, suffered as a result of the direct or indirect use or application of any
element of the contents of this work. Patient names have been changed to protect privacy.

Greystone Books gratefully acknowledges the Musqueam, Squamish,
and Tsleil-Waututh peoples on whose land our office is located.

Greystone Books thanks the Canada Council for the Arts, the British Columbia Arts
Council, the Province of British Columbia through the Book Publishing Tax Credit, and
the Government of Canada for supporting our publishing activities.

CONTENTS

Step 6

ALL IN YOUR HEAD?

Sexual Fantasies   *83*

Step 7

SWING IT!

The Pelvic Swing   *95*

Step 8

BE MORE SELF-CENTERED!

Pay Attention to You   *109*

Step 9

SWING IT TOGETHER!

Movement in Duet   *119*

Step 10

BLASTING OFF TOGETHER

A Lifetime of Good Sex   *129*

INTRODUCTION

S HE TAKES A big sip of red wine, sets the glass back down on the table a bit too quickly, spilling almost half of it—it's her third—and while wiping the table with her paper napkin she says, without looking up, "Okay, tell me the secret!" Laura and I have known each other since our school days. After high school we went our separate ways: she studied law and I psychology, and the red wine and pizza evenings became fewer and farther between, but we've never lost touch.

"What secret?" I ask. Laura takes a bite of pizza and says quickly, without swallowing, "I want to know how to have an orgasm during sex. Just with in-and-out sex, I mean. Like normal women. It doesn't work for me. It just doesn't work! I must be broken! I think something's broken down there!"

Laura says she doesn't know what to do. She and her boyfriend have slept together in every possible way—fast and slow, tender and hard—but it just doesn't bring her to orgasm.

It's pretty common for my friends to ask me their sex questions over a glass of wine. They have to get over their shyness first, they often say. I'm a sexologist, after all. Talking about sex with me is like showing a professional photographer your smartphone snapshots.

But when women—like Laura—get over their bashfulness, they always feel tremendously relieved. Because I can reassure Laura and everyone else who can't come "just like that" during sex. They're not broken. They're not even the exception. "It's like that for millions of women," I explain, and Laura breathes out with a sigh, as if a great weight had just been lifted from her shoulders.

The thing that bothers Laura also plagues many of the women that come to me for sex therapy. Lack of orgasm through sex, difficulty achieving orgasm, and the low sex drive that often accompanies these issues are the most common topics women come to me to talk about. Since so many women have the same questions, I've started leading a regular orgasm group with my colleague Annette Bischof-Campbell. In the group, women spend several evenings together getting to know their bodies better and learning how they can gain more pleasure from sex, increase their potential to orgasm, and separate orgasm myths from reality. The group has many advantages: we can introduce a lot of people to the topic at the same time, and among their peers, women come to realize that they're not alone with their problems. In addition, they can benefit from each other's discoveries and successes. We've also noticed again and again that women come to the group who say they actually don't "need" sex therapy, but that there's nonetheless something they'd like to explore.

The orgasm group is one of the highlights of my week. It always makes me so happy to see how many new ideas our discussions spark among the women. Yet I'm also always astounded to see how much ignorance there is around the topic of female orgasm, and how much nonsense has taken root in the minds of many women.

I realized how neglected the topic of sex was when I had my first boyfriend, during puberty. Luckily, I have a wonderful and very open mother, and I could ask her all my questions about sex and my body—aside from her, there was no one with whom I could have talked about such things. Sex ed in school was the opposite of practical and positive, and though wild stories of first times circulated among my girlfriends, we couldn't have any serious conversations about sex.

Even during my studies in psychology I learned very little about sexuality. But I was already convinced that sex and desire have a great influence on the psyche, and so I decided to research the topic further for my thesis. I went to my professor with a proposal to write about sexual behavior in Switzerland. His reaction was cautious, and he finally agreed through gritted teeth that I could write about it if I found five hundred participants for the required online survey. An astonishing fifteen thousand respondents later, I got his go-ahead—and realized that I wanted to be a sex therapist. I wanted to somehow counter the great silence that surrounded sex. And the fact that fifteen thousand people took the time to fill out my survey goes to show how great the general interest in sex is.

Since 2008, I've had my own practice as a psychotherapist and sexologist, and I'm passionate about my job—I love helping women, men, and couples to communicate better and get more enjoyment out of their relationships and sex lives. Today, I'm married with two children, and it still seems to me that sexuality is not a much discussed topic, especially for women. It's high time that we get to know and understand our bodies better instead of relying on years or even decades of dubious half-knowledge gathered from so-called women's magazines. For in fact, a lot is written about the female orgasm, and countless myths and legends circulate about it. Probably the most common myth is that women can come either vaginally or clitorally. Some are supposedly blessed with the ability to reach orgasm simply through penetration—and others aren't. Is it just chance? Luck? Anatomy? Is it mental? A matter of relaxation? Meaning: If you can't let go, you won't reach climax? Spoiler alert: it's all nonsense! It's very important to understand that even the so-called vaginal orgasm—the one triggered by penetration—usually comes from stimulation of both the vagina *and* the clitoris. But more on that later.

The female orgasm often provokes questions. And it's not rare for young, curious, liberated women like my friend Laura to imagine there is a "secret" to it. On that wine-soaked evening I said to her, "The secret is that there is no secret. Coming through sex is a matter of practice. You're anything but broken. You probably just have to train yourself."

Right away, Laura had a thousand questions. Over our next glass of wine, I explained to her the things that are now contained in this book. It's very important to me to empower women to engage intensively with their bodies and their sexuality. Because sex can be learned. Desire, too.

Every woman can have great orgasms. Getting to know your body pays off, because you can profit from it for the rest of your life.

Orgasm isn't a matter of good or bad luck, fate, or the right kind of relaxation, but rather of abilities that all women have, but some have yet to develop. In fact, very few women come to orgasm through penis-in-vagina sex alone—only about thirty percent often or always climax this way. About sixty percent of women don't find penetration per se very sexually arousing. That's a shame, because coming through vaginal stimulation can be highly enjoyable, and it can be learned.

It's incredible how few people know this. There's a very simple biological explanation for this kind of orgasm: every part of the body is equipped with nerve cells and sensors that are connected to the brain through nerve pathways. When these nerve cells are touched and used, more connections are made with the neurons in the brain. The stronger these pathways, the quicker the brain reacts when the body part is touched, and the more intense the sensation will be. (In this book, we'll refer to this process as *sensitizing*: learning to become more fully aware of the sensations in the vagina and connecting them to a feeling of arousal, thereby fully inhabiting this part of your body.) Since some women haven't established a strong vagina-brain connection, they feel little during sex.

In that case, the vagina simply isn't trained—it hasn't yet been "woken up" and connected with a feeling of lust. In order for it to be responsive, we have to develop the connection. Take a ballerina, for example. She practices her steps for months. The region in her brain corresponding to her feet will be more active than that of a person who doesn't dance. In the same way, a pianist doesn't have to look at her hands when she plays: over time, her fingertips have become well-connected with the brain, and they find the right keys on their own.

The principle of practice also applies to the vagina. Every woman can activate this area through touching, thereby triggering changes in the brain and developing stronger feelings of arousal. Which in turn means: it's possible for all women to reach climax through penetration alone. But some training is necessary, or more precisely: a ten-step program. The knowledge and exercises you need can be found right in this book.

The fact that so few people know that the female orgasm is a matter of practice is the result, in my opinion, of two things: First, women's orgasms have only recently become the subject of serious research. For a long time, they weren't a focus because, from a strictly biological per-spective, the female orgasm is unnecessary. The woman doesn't need to have an orgasm to become pregnant. While female orgasm may boost chances of conception, it isn't required for procreation to occur.

Secondly, the term *training* is probably nowhere so jar-ring as in the context of sex. No one wants to train, or to have to "work at" sex. Especially since it seems the deck is already stacked against women. No one has to train his penis in order to come, right?

Well, that's not exactly true. The penis has to "prac-tice" too, only usually boys do this during childhood and adolescence. It's much easier for a little boy to awaken the connections with his sex parts because they are easier to touch and see than those of a little girl. The penis is touched early and in many situations: when peeing or putting on pants, for example, and most boys learn to associate their penises with pleasurable feelings from a very young age. Women are at a disadvantage here, since the vagina is inside the body. And it's covered—among other things, by shame. Did you know that the term for women's genitalia, *pudenda*, also means "something to be ashamed of" in Latin? That says a lot. If a little girl touches herself between the legs, she's often reprimanded by her parents. But if a boy plays with his penis, the parents simply think: he's doing what all boys do.

The result is that the vagina may remain untouched during the early years of a woman's life. At some point, it might come into contact with tampons, whose insertion is anything but pleasurable. And then a young woman has sex. The famous, much-touted first time. Perhaps she finds it nice, and exciting. Or painful. But she probably doesn't find it particularly pleasurable. How could she? The nerve endings in her vagina have never been associated with pleasure, so they can't feel much yet. Years later, she might find that there's rarely time for long, indulgent sex: because of work, because of children, because she and her partner have different interests. And who gets shortchanged when there's no fore-, inter-, or afterplay? Usually the woman. If this continues long term, she'll eventually lose interest and desire. Because intercourse, the simple in-and-out, doesn't physically do much for her.

And so it's very important for women to communicate to their partners what arouses them—what techniques they've already learned through masturbation for increasing arousal and maybe even reaching orgasm. Often, it's deliberate stimulation of the clitoris. In this case, the woman can take matters into her own hands, or show her partner how she'd like to be touched.

Greater vaginal sensitivity isn't essential, but it's an exciting bonus. You can have terrific sex without it: an orgasm that's caused by stimulation of the tip of the clitoris is great, and very satisfying. In this case, the woman doesn't come through penetration, but rather is brought to orgasm before, during, or after penetration with a hand, vibrator, or mouth. That's exciting and gratifying all by itself.

But when you also learn to be more vaginally arousable, your sex life will grow more varied. It can be exciting and satisfying in a different way, because you can control your arousal yourself rather than being dependent on your partner doing everything a particular way. Because you can choose when to have your orgasm. Because your desire for sex will grow. Because it's sometimes nice to come together. And because it feels wonderful to be able to reach climax through intercourse with your partner.

This book will help you get to know your body better, help you recognize how you come to orgasm through penetration or why you haven't yet, and show you the relationship between fantasy, pleasure, desire, and arousal. In each of the ten steps, frequently asked questions will be answered and specific exercises suggested. Each topic is also accompanied by a case study from my practice. At the end of the book, you'll find tips for men, as well as for female partners—because your partner can learn and practice too if you want to blast off together.

(Step 1)

MINI ANATOMY LESSON

The Vagina, Vulva, and Clitoris

F YOU WANT to feel more during sex, you should get to know your vulva and vagina better. You can sit down and do a self-exam with a mirror if you want to, but it's much more important to understand your body through your "inner sense." You can do this best through your own perception: by touching yourself, investigating with your fingers, and thereby "grasping" yourself—like a child discovering the world. You see your body from the outside in the mirror or in photos, but you probably don't pay so much attention to how it feels. If you rarely intentionally feel your own body, it can start to feel very foreign. That's a shame, because your "inner sense" can learn what feels good to you and can guide you to do the things that will do you and your body good.

When you lack this internal gauge, you have to rely more on external factors to get a sense of your body. External standards might be photos of models, a friend's appearance, the pounds on your scale, or the calorie count of food—everything, in other words, that you see, hear, and read. These standards have very little to do with you, however, and they may even put you under unneces-sary pressure: your body has its own unique shape and qualities—and that makes it perfect! That's why I suggest getting to know your body through your internal percep-tion, using your fingers as a guide while you take this trip through your own anatomy.

The vulva:
What you can see from the outside

THE VULVA IS the part of the female sex organs that's visible from outside: it starts from the pubic mound and ends behind the entrance to the vagina. Behind that is the perineum and anus. In the first step it's important to find out where you stand, personally: what you can already do, what you already know, and where there's room to learn.

Pick up a pencil and a clean sheet of paper. Try drawing your vulva and labeling the parts. Don't worry if you're not sure: over half of women don't know where to find the opening of the urethra, for example.

Now draw your vulva again after feeling every inch of it—as if there were eyes on your fingertips working their way forward bit by tiny bit.

Let's take a closer look at the vulva:

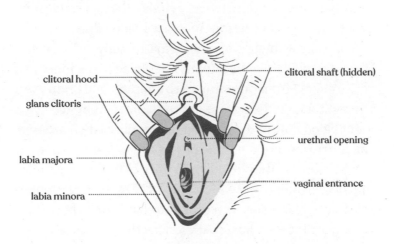

Compare this drawing to yours. Is the clitoris approximately in the same place? The urethra? The labia? There is a wide range of "normal" when it comes to vulvas, so not everyone will be exactly the same.

The labia are often referred to as vaginal lips, or simply lips. They're also often spoken of in terms of outer and inner lips, which can be somewhat confusing—as the "inner" lips are often larger than the "outer" ones and can extend beyond them. This is nothing to be ashamed of—and the trend of surgically reducing the size of the inner lips is actually quite dangerous: injury or scarring from the procedure can cause numbness. And an area that's numb—obviously—can't feel anything. Not to mention the possibility of pain resulting from the procedure.

Though their names are similar, the inner and outer labia have different qualities and functions. The outer labia are basically fat pads that protect our private parts and the underlying bones from external pressure. They're covered with hair and contain sweat glands. They usually grow darker during arousal from increased blood flow.

For some women, the inner labia are only visible when the outer ones are pulled apart. The shape of the inner lips varies greatly from one woman to another, and often even the right and left sides are different sizes. They receive a lot of blood flow and can swell perceptibly when aroused. The inner labia are much thinner and more sensitive than the outer ones. They're covered with skin that resembles mucous membranes, which means they lack the outer-most layer that other types of skin have, and they don't grow hair. These characteristics make them more sensitive, so touching the inner lips often feels very good.

The clitoris: Bigger than you think

THE CLITORIS IS significantly bigger than the little knob you can see as part of the vulva. The whole thing measures a good three inches! It comprises the visible tip and its foreskin, which looks like a hood; the shaft; and the two crura (the "legs" of the clitoris; the singular is *crus*). These reach deep into the body and surround the entrance to the vagina.

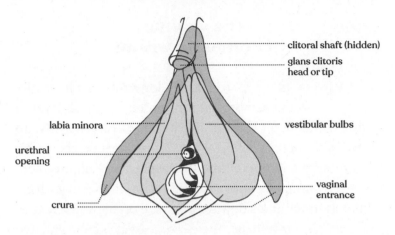

clitoral shaft (hidden)

glans clitoris
head or tip

labia minora

vestibular bulbs

urethral
opening

vaginal
entrance

crura

The whole clitoris contains vast numbers of nerve cells, yet for many women only the small, visible part is sensitized. This has to do with the fact that the glans (the tip) is particularly dense with all kinds of friction receptors, making it particularly sensitive. Therefore, some women learn to turn themselves on by rubbing, stroking, or pushing on the external, and very sensitive, glans of the clitoris. Others find direct contact with this extremely sensitive place rather unpleasant, and prefer to arouse themselves by rubbing the surrounding areas.

When a woman is aroused, the clitoris gets bigger, since it—just like the penis—is made up of erectile tissue. This means that it fills with blood and swells. The glans and shaft actually become erect, and the vestibule of the vagina expands. The degree to which the glans and shaft become enlarged varies from woman to woman. The head of the clitoris has up to eight thousand nerve and sensory cells—twice as many as the head of the penis!

The vagina:
The marvel within

THE VAGINA IS a 2.5- to 5-inch-long tube made of very elastic mucous membrane surrounded by a thin layer of muscle. The outer third of the vagina is very sensitive to touch and friction, whereas farther inside it reacts mostly to pressure and stretching. Therefore, women are more aroused during sex when the vagina is stimulated with circular motions and sideways pressure on its walls than by in-and-out movement. The cervix can also be stimulated through touch. This spot deep within the vagina predictably also reacts most strongly to pressure and stretching. So when a woman lies quietly during sex and her partner primarily moves in and out, it's often not terribly exciting for the vagina. It gets much more interesting when one of the partners, or—better—both, make rocking motions and move their pelvis in circles, massaging the walls of the vagina. There will be more on this later in the book. First, let's look a bit more closely at a non-aroused vagina:

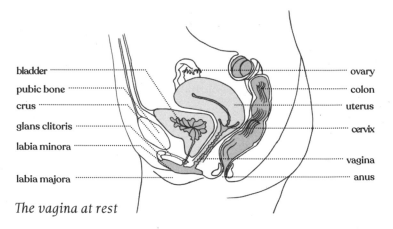

bladder ·········· ovary
pubic bone ·········· colon
crus ·········· uterus
glans clitoris ·········· cervix
labia minora ··········
·········· vagina
labia majora ·········· anus

The vagina at rest

In the vagina's resting state, its walls touch each other, so from the outside it doesn't look like an open tunnel. Yet the vagina is so flexible and can expand so much that a baby can fit through it in childbirth. Even unaroused, the vagina is moist, since the cervix secretes a fluid that keeps it and the vagina clean and healthy. The vagina is surrounded by the muscles of the pelvic floor. With your finger, you can feel the sphincter muscles, up to three-quarters of an inch inside the vagina, on both sides. These can be tensed: when you want to want to stop a stream of urine, for example. Farther inside, the vagina is surrounded by deeper levels of muscles. During orgasm, these muscles repeatedly contract, involuntarily and rhythmically. If you feel pain or fear, the muscles of the pelvic floor tend to tense severely, leading to the feeling that the vagina is too narrow for sex.

When aroused, the vagina looks different. The vagina secretes a clear fluid and its walls become wet. This fluid also moistens the vulva and clitoris, which eases the entry of the penis, or fingers or a sex toy, and helps sperm travel to the uterus. In addition, the vagina balloons—it tips upward and expands in order to receive the penis:

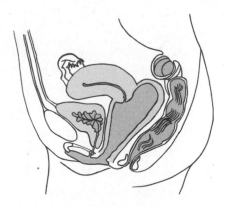

The aroused vagina

WHEN YOU INSERT your finger into your vagina, you might feel a ridged surface on the front wall. This is where you'll find the G-spot, about two inches from the entrance. In fact, the G-spot isn't so much a "spot" as a surface about the size of a quarter. It should really be called the G-surface or G-zone. The G, by the way, stands for "Gräfenberg," the name of the man who discovered it. The G-zone is still highly debated—scientists don't agree on exactly what or where it is, or even whether it exists at all—but many women report having pleasurable sensations from this area.

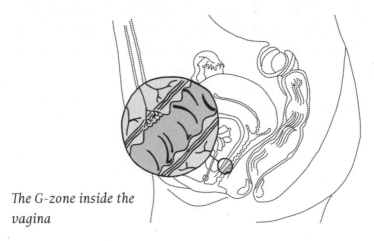

The G-zone inside the vagina

The G-zone is made of clitoral erectile tissue that lies near the urethra. When you touch this tissue for the first time, you'll probably have the sensation of needing to pee. This is because the G-zone is located close to the urethra, and we need to learn to distinguish sensations in the G-zone from sensations in the urethra. Through practice, you can learn to tell the difference between them and to find one arousing. In fact, this is even one way to reach orgasm.

But the G-zone is far from the only part of the vagina that can be aroused—even though this is what we're often led to believe. In fact, the back and side walls of the vagina, the cervix, and also, indirectly, the pelvic musculature, are full of different kinds of receptors. The whole vagina contains nerve endings and can therefore be sensitized.

Proper care of the vulva and vagina

MANY WOMEN DON'T know how to properly care for their sex parts. Yet care of the vulva and vagina—and the appreciation that goes along with it—are important when it comes to building a good relationship with your own sex parts. Try it!

Here are a few simple tips:

* Don't use soap on the vulva or in the vagina! Water alone is enough. You also shouldn't use shower gel, because it can disturb the natural flora, which can in turn lead to infection. Feminine hygiene washes, scented sprays, and deodorants are also unnecessary and can irritate your vagina and vulva.

* You don't have to wash out your vagina: it "cleans" itself.

* The skin of your intimate regions likes to be pampered after bathing. You can moisturize your vulva just as you do your face and legs, though avoid using any products with scents or chemical additives. The best option is a

neutral, unscented oil (for example, almond, olive, or coconut oil). If you use condoms, you have to be careful, as oils can make them porous and ineffective. Vaseline isn't a good choice—it doesn't let your skin breathe.

* To avoid UTIS and yeast infections, always urinate after sex—you can go right back to bed afterward. Remember: "After sex" means ten minutes, max—no later!

* If you're prone to vaginal infections, use a vaginal gel with a low pH.

* For more tips, ask your gynecologist.

THE SAME BASIC principle applies to the skin of your sex parts as to the skin on the rest of your body: it needs moisture and simple care. Because the skin there is thinner and more sensitive, it's especially important to avoid fragrances and chemical additives. A positive side effect of moisturizing is that you'll become more and more familiar with your sex parts and get to know them better. If you want, you can smell your fingers or put them in your mouth after touching yourself—this is also part of getting to know your body. If this sounds strange to you, just think how often you put your fingers in your mouth when they're not freshly washed—you come into contact with far more harmful bacteria in this way than by touching your own body.

About the exercises
in this book

EACH OF THE ten chapters in this book includes a set of exercises to help you put into practice what you've learned in the chapter. How often should you do these exercises? The same principle applies here as when you're learning a musical instrument: the body needs a lot of repetition to be able to really integrate what's learned into its repertoire. Therefore, it's more useful to practice more often for shorter periods than once a week for hours. You can repeat the exercises of each step for one week or several, until you feel comfortable with them—it's just a question of how quickly your body learns. For each exercise you can either set a time limit (one to twenty minutes) or turn on some music and practice for the length of two or three songs. The crucial thing is to devote your full attention to what you're doing rather than constantly watching the clock or letting your attention wander.

If you're impatient and want to make quick progress, you can also get through the exercises of the ten steps fairly quickly. There's no "right" way—and you can always go back a step or two if you feel that you've gone too quickly and haven't explored as much as you'd like. It's your choice: if you want to satisfy your curiosity first and try out all the exercises before returning to the ones where you feel you need more practice, that's fine too!

Exercises

1. Touch your vulva and vagina several times a week. How? First, let's try a warm-up exercise. Make a loose fist with your left hand to represent your sex parts. Slowly insert your right index finger: What do you feel? Where is it soft? Where is it warm? Are there rough spots? Now try the same thing with your vagina, first touching around your vulva and then slowly inserting a finger when you're ready, and ask yourself the same questions. Focus on what your finger touches rather than on what your vagina feels. Ultimately, the idea is to discover what your vulva and vagina feel like. If you're not used to touching yourself in this way, try to smile while you're doing the exercise. This will trigger positive emotions in your brain, which will in turn make the exercise easier.

2. Think as precisely as possible about how you feel arousal. Try this while you're doing the exercise above, and also when you're not touching yourself. Where do you feel the arousal? What does it feel like? Do you really physically feel something, or does it happen more on an emotional level? Do you feel arousal differently when you're touching yourself compared to when you're not? Many women find it hard to describe their arousal in words and sometimes don't even notice when they're

aroused, even though their bodies show signs of it. Try to pay close attention to the tiny changes that happen to your sex parts.

Good to know

Why do I have to touch myself? Can't I just take a picture or use a mirror? That would also show me what my vulva looks like.

Your fingers can give you a very different kind of feedback. There's a reason people talk about "grasping" something when they mean really understanding it. And eyes can be tough critics. When you touch yourself, you're feeling the same places that you're trying to sensitize—so this is the beginning of the work to "wake up" those areas.

My clitoris and vagina are fairly far apart. If they were closer together, would that make it more likely for me to have an orgasm during penetration? Is it a question of anatomy after all?

Yes and no. The tip of a woman's clitoris is very sensitive, and if she often arouses herself clitorally, then there's a strong connection between clitoris and brain. If this highly sensitized clitoris happens to lie close enough to the vagina and she has sex in a position that causes it to feel a lot of friction, then she may well come to orgasm through sexual intercourse. If the tip of her clitoris is far from the vagina, it probably won't feel a lot during sex. But if we strengthen the connection to the vagina, it no longer matters how close the tip of the clitoris is—because the crura of the clitoris inside the vagina, among other things, have been better sensitized.

If the clitoris surrounds the vagina, then there's really no such thing as a "vaginal orgasm," right?

Whether the clitoral legs, the G-spot, the cervix, the urethral opening, or the entire inner wall of the vagina is most sensitive to contact varies from woman to woman. In their 2004 study, the neuroscientist Barry Komisaruk and his colleagues refuted the idea that the female orgasm always derives from the clitoris: women with complete paraplegia were not brought to orgasm through stimulation of the clitoris yet could experience orgasm with stimulation of the vagina and cervix. This is possible because impulses from the clitoris are transmitted to the brain through the spinal cord, whereas from the cervix they're transmitted via the vagus nerve, which does not run through the spinal cord. This nervous pathway is not interrupted in paraplegic women. There is therefore a form of female orgasm that can be triggered through the vagina.

For most women, though, orgasm usually comes about through a combination of clitoral and vaginal stimulation. So no matter what, the principle holds: the more areas that are sensitized—from the clitoris to the entrance to the vagina, from the G-zone and vaginal walls to the cervix—the more a woman will feel during sex. Then her orgasm will be triggered by arousal in several areas. In this book, we're referring to this as an internal orgasm, an orgasm from penetration, or an orgasm from vaginal stimulation. Of course, the whole of the clitoris is in fact also involved. But some women who've already experienced these types of orgasms say that an orgasm triggered primarily by stimulation of the vagina feels more all-encompassing. An orgasm triggered by clitoral stimulation is often felt most strongly around the clitoris itself, while an internal orgasm can be felt in the whole body. Women who stimulate both the clitoris and the vagina describe their orgasms as particularly full and intense, as Kerstin Fugl-Meyer and her colleagues established in a 2006 article in the *Journal of Sexual Medicine*.

What's squirting? How does it happen in the body?

Some women emit large volumes of fluid when they come. This is informally called *squirting*. When a woman stimulates herself or is stimulated in the G-zone through pressure on the area, it's possible for fluid to squirt out of the urinary opening. Usually when this happens, a woman will tense her pelvic muscles, and if she's really intensely aroused, she may briefly lose control of the muscles that close the urethra. The contraction of the pelvic muscles can shoot out watery fluid, together with a milky secretion from the female prostate. (Researchers usually distinguish between *female ejaculation*—expelling this secretion from the female prostate alone—and *squirting*—expelling a larger amount of liquid from the bladder along with the secretion.) The phenomenon has yet to be really thoroughly researched.

Some women find this very arousing, to be able to "completely let go." The squirting or ejaculation can happen at the same time as the orgasm, but doesn't have to. If you squirt and don't want your mattress to get soaked, you can simply lay towels on the bed.

Susanne

SUSANNE IS TWENTY-TWO AND comes to me because she and her boyfriend keep having discussions—almost fights—on the topic of oral sex. He'd like to have more of it. He enjoys going down on her and likes it when she gives him a blowjob. She does both only reluctantly. Susanne says that she does find oral sex arousing, but the situation usually just makes her uncomfortable. "It's only okay when I've just showered," she says. She can't believe that her boyfriend actually likes to do it. She thinks he's just saying so because he doesn't want her to feel insecure, and because he expects something from her in return. When he's going down on her, all she can think about is what a chore it must be for him. Her boyfriend is annoyed and thinks she's being difficult. This puts a strain on the relationship. Susanne wants to change something, even if it's "not a big deal." She just doesn't want oral sex to become a long-term issue between them.

It seems to me that Susanne has anxiety about her sex parts. I ask her if she knows what her genitals look like—if she's ever looked carefully. She says she's looked, but doesn't think she's very attractive "down there." Her inner labia are longer than her outer ones, and they stick out in a way that she finds very embarrassing. She also thinks that her vagina sometimes smells bad, so she uses a feminine hygiene wash, which doesn't really help.

While she's talking, she realizes how weird and unattractive she actually finds her sex parts. I tell her that many women have larger labia minora—in fact, at least half of women, according to some studies—and that it's completely normal. Then I give her some tips on getting to know her sex parts better. I recommend that she really touch herself when she showers, rather than just rinsing off without looking. I also suggest that she put oil on her genitals after showering, inside and out. That way she can "look" with her fingers. I tell her not to focus on looking at her genitals with her eyes, which can lead to too much focus on appearance, especially for women who are prone to be critical about their bodies. In Susanne's case, the goal is to learn to smell, taste, and touch herself better, step-by-step. The more Susanne feels, accepts, and likes herself, the easier it will be for her to accept that someone else could feel the same way. She'll become less skeptical when her boyfriend tells her he likes oral sex.

Of course, this doesn't mean that she has to have and like oral sex. All of my patients have their own needs. It's important for me to address concerns individually rather than reinforcing norms. In the end, there's nothing that a patient has to do or like. I tell Susanne that she absolutely shouldn't force herself to do something, but that if she likes the idea of oral sex, then she can try to be more open to it.

Susanne says that in theory she really likes oral sex and would like to be able to enjoy it more. Over the next weeks, she comes to see me regularly, and through our sessions she's gradually able to get over her embarrassment about her sex parts. She can perceive touch more strongly and feels more easily aroused. There's also an automatic side benefit: as Susanne gets over her anxiety about her own body, she'll have more positive feelings about her boyfriend's penis and will be able to enjoy giving oral sex more.

Six months later, she comes to see me and tells me she likes it better every time her boyfriend goes down on her. She rarely wonders what he's thinking while he's at it, since she's concentrating on her own sensations and trusting him. And now she believes him when he tells her he really enjoys oral sex with her.

(Step 2)

WHERE DO I STAND?

My Body and What I Like

BEFORE WE GET deeper into our subject, it's important to understand that sex, like so many other things, is a matter of practice. If you want to learn French, you have to learn vocabulary. If you want to run a marathon, you have to get in shape. If you want to play piano well, you have to practice. If you want to be good at anything, you have to learn how—you apply this principle to everything in your life. Except sex—somehow in bed we expect everything to happen automatically. It never occurs to us to practice. We always hear about women for whom sex "just works." But this is a misconception. Either these women aren't being entirely honest, or they simply don't realize how much they've practiced—perhaps because it felt quite natural to them. It's also important to understand that sex encompasses a whole range of activities—including self-pleasuring, and all kinds of play with one partner or more—rather than just sexual intercourse with a partner. This book focuses specifically on learning to have an orgasm through vaginal penetration, but by no means should that be taken to suggest that this is the be-all and end-all of sex—to the contrary, it is only one particular expression of sexuality.

As has already been described, every part of the body is connected to the brain through nerve pathways. Scientific evidence shows that the pathways we consistently use become stronger. When we don't activate these pathways, however, the connection to the brain will be as bumpy as a country road, and few synapses will be formed in the corresponding area of the brain. When, for example, a woman is used to arousing herself solely through touching the clitoris, this will reliably bring her to orgasm. She may hardly feel anything when her vagina is stimulated, however, and therefore won't enjoy penetration—she simply hasn't learned to connect her sense of arousal to her vagina. The untraveled country roads and the unused areas of her brain have to be activated and developed through repetition.

It's simple: sex works just the way everything else does. Unfortunately. Or fortunately! If it weren't so, lots of women would simply be unlucky, and there would be nothing they could do to change the fact that they don't come to orgasm through intercourse.

Some parts of our body are naturally more sensitive than others; our lips and fingertips, for example, have more sensory receptors than other body parts, and larger corresponding regions in the cortex of the brain. While we can't change the number of receptors we have, through training we can learn to use them to their full potential. The more we become aware of these connections and use them, the more precisely we can locate the source of our sensations. For example, if something touches your ring finger, you know exactly which finger is being touched. If something touches the middle toe of your right foot, you might not be one hundred percent certain which toe it was. Our toes simply aren't as sensitive as our fingers, and because we focus our attention on them less often, their connection with our brain isn't as precise. The same goes for your sex parts—the vulva and vagina.

Your sex parts have many, many nerve endings. Some of them react to rubbing or stroking, some to pressure, and others to vibration. If such stimulation occurs, nerve impulses are sent to the brain from that part of the body. When we touch a part of the body that is not used to stimulation, we might feel little, or we might even feel uncomfortable. The brain has not yet formed associations with this kind of touch. The more connections the brain makes with an area of the body, the more responsive that area will become.

How does nerve conduction work, exactly? With every touch, an impulse is sent from the place being touched to the brain. In the cerebral cortex, and more specifically the somatosensory cortex, different regions are responsible for sensations in different parts of the body.

Some body parts get more space than others in the cerebral cortex. The oft-used (and very sensitive) lips and thumbs have larger areas than, for example, the hips or neck, which we actively use more rarely. The proportions of the rather unshapely person in the following graphic demonstrate this idea: the bigger the body part is shown, the more space it's given in our brains.

Allocation of space in the somatosensory cortex of the cerebral cortex to parts of the body

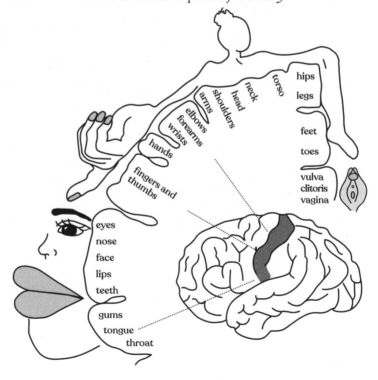

THE REGION FOR the sex organs lies in the central sulcus (or groove) at the top of the brain. In order for us to have a full response when these parts are stimulated, synapses first have to form in the cerebral cortex. Synapses are connections between individual nerve cells, responsible for storing and quickly relaying information. They form all the time in our brain, passing a signal from one nerve cell to the next and stabilizing the more these connections are used. When the nerve endings of sex parts or other parts of the body send impulses to the correlating areas of the brain frequently enough, the synapses will become stronger.

One of the reasons that many women don't come to orgasm through stimulation of the vagina is thus that the vagina-brain connection isn't yet as strong as it could be. The brain has not connected the stimulation it receives there to arousal. For some women, only a small part of the vulva is highly sensitive and capable of feeling arousal. Usually this is the clitoris, and often only the small, externally visible part of it: the tip. Because its nerve endings are particularly sensitive, and it's the part most frequently touched when we're aroused, the corresponding synapses in the cerebral cortex are well trained. The brain has thus learned to like this method of producing and increasing arousal. On the other hand, this means that parts of the body that aren't stimulated as often won't be as responsive.

Our brains may not immediately respond to a new kind of stimulation as intensely or in the way we expect or desire. In order for new synapses to form in the brain, connections have to be strengthened over time, which might mean consciously touching the vagina thousands of times! But don't panic: this doesn't mean that you have to practice thousands of times—if that were so, we'd never get anywhere. Every time you practice, you touch any given spot many hundreds of times. This means that every time you practice, you'll be able to sense a change in your body. Some people will feel a continuous change, while for others it will take a while to sense, but then the effect will be that much stronger. Every woman works a bit differently. If you stick to it, you'll be rewarded—guaranteed!

Before you start, you have to find out which connections you already have. In order to know what exactly you want to train, you also have to know which areas are already working well. Where are your "strengths"? You have to know your own patterns of arousal very well if you want to broaden your repertoire. Pay close attention to your feelings and sensations. Where do you feel a lot? Which places are already well connected to the brain? What kinds of stimulation do you react to? What has to happen in order for you to come to orgasm? If you feel little when you touch your vagina: What minor variations can you sense? Which places give you a more pleasant feeling than others?

If you want to know more about the various types and methods of arousal, you can find more in the chapter "Theory for the Knowledge Seeker: The Four Types of Arousal" near the end of the book. You don't need to know this more theoretical background to do the next steps, but in this chapter, you'll find fascinating insights into the topic, if it's something that interests you.

Take a survey of the way you arouse yourself and bring yourself to orgasm. The following questions might help.

THE ORGASM QUESTIONNAIRE—SOLO

How do I do it?

* Do I regularly pleasure myself?
* When I do masturbate, what's the usual position of my body?
* What tools do I use: hand, vibrator, pillow, etc.?
* How do I touch myself? How many fingers do I use? In which direction do I move them? Right? Or more to the left?
* Where exactly do I touch myself?
* What kind of rhythm do I use? Slow or fast?
* How much pressure or tension do I use?
* Do I squeeze my legs together?
* How fast do I breathe?
* How do I move my body?
* What images, fantasies, and thoughts do I use?
* What do I think about when I start? What do I think about right before orgasm?
* How long does it take before I come?
* What do I usually do or change right before the climax in order to bring myself over the edge?
* Do I have different fantasies at that point? Do I rub faster, harder?
* How long does the orgasm last?
* And how long does it take for me to come down afterward?

Now, let's take a look at sex with a partner:

THE ORGASM QUESTIONNAIRE—TOGETHER

How do we do it?

* What turns me on?
* What kinds of touch increase my arousal?
* What kinds of touch decrease it?
* What distracts or disturbs me during sex?
* In which positions do we have sex?
* In which position do I feel the most? In which position do I feel the least?
* What do I feel?
* Do I find intercourse arousing?
* Do I find other activities arousing, like kissing or giving or receiving oral sex?
* Do I or does my partner stimulate my clitoris during sex?
* Do I like it fast or slow?
* Does my arousal increase with speed?
* Am I tense?
* Do I move?
* Do I like it hard, or more on the gentle side?
* Do I always like it the same way, or does it depend?
* What are my reactions to my partner's genitals and body?
* Does my partner distract me from my arousal?
* How important is it for my partner to do the exact right thing?
* Do I get closer to orgasm in a particular position?
* Is there a position that causes me pain?

THESE QUESTIONNAIRES CAN help you figure out what excites you sexually, and how strong your enjoyment of these things is. This is important, because it will help you to recognize what you've already learned and which parts of your body are already sensitized. It's also interesting that many women realize through this exercise that they stimulate different areas and use different techniques when they masturbate than during sex with a partner.

This, in turn, can help us to understand that enjoyment and physical arousal aren't necessarily the same thing. Sex can be very enjoyable and pleasurable even with only moderate physical arousal. Conversely, a woman can be very aroused and yet not feel much on an emotional level. Enjoyment and physical arousal are two factors that don't always go hand in hand.

For example: Nina wants to relax, so she turns on her vibrator. She holds it on the right side of her clitoris and cranks it all the way up. It takes two minutes. She comes. Her body was aroused, at least by the end, or she wouldn't have come. It wasn't tremendously enjoyable, but the goal was to tune out, and she was interested in the relaxation that comes after orgasm rather than primarily in pleasure. If one were to diagram the two factors as a curve, it would look approximately like the chart on the next page: the curve of physical arousal, shown in black, rises quickly, has its peak in the orgasm, and then quickly falls. The emotional pleasure/enjoyment curve, drawn in grey, looks different: it rises less and more slowly, but is at its highest point after the orgasm, during the phase of relaxation—then it falls precipitously. It's never really very high to begin with.

Diagram of Nina's arousal during masturbation

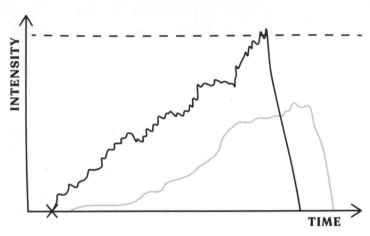

An example of the progression of arousal during masturbation

ANOTHER EXAMPLE: NOW Nina has long, indulgent sex with her boyfriend. First they make out, then he goes down on her. They have sex in the missionary position and then he takes her from behind, until he comes. Nina doesn't have an orgasm, but she enjoyed the sex very much. She was very aroused, and loved the intimacy and closeness she felt to her partner. She felt not so much in the first position, then a bit more in the second, but she had a lot of fun in spite of it. The curve of her physical arousal (black) starts high and rises more during oral sex, then plateaus and falls to its lowest point during penetration. The curve of enjoyment is high the whole time, even during penetration.

Diagram of Nina's arousal during sex

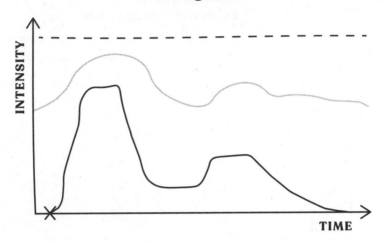

An example of the progression of arousal during sex with a partner

The two curves—physical arousal and emotional enjoyment—progress differently in both examples. Next, we'll address more specifically why it's important to be able to tell the difference between physical sexual arousal and the perception of arousal.

But first, let's chart your personal curves of arousal. Using two different-colored pens, use the following diagrams to sketch your physical sexual arousal and your enjoyment. The first color shows what your body feels: just your body. If your body likes a particular kind of stimulation, the curve will rise. The second color stands for what you experience, and how much you enjoy the sex. If you find it nice, sensual, exciting, hot, or simply good, this curve will rise.

Masturbation 1
(when it has to happen fast)

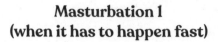
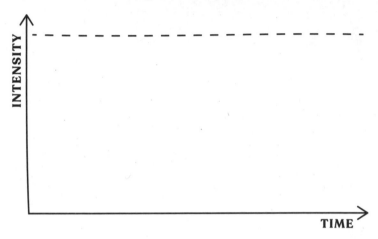

Masturbation 2
(when you take your time)

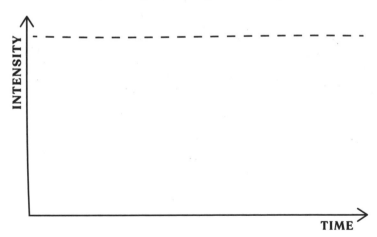

Sex with a partner 1
(quick sex, primarily penetration)

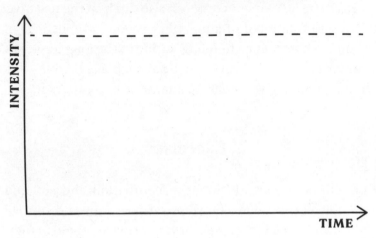

Sex with a partner 2
(long sex with plenty of variety)

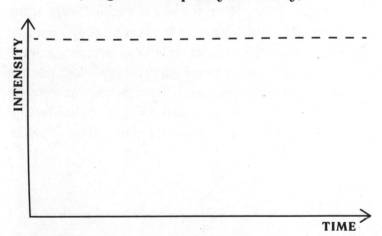

FOR MOST OF us, our arousal and enjoyment curves will rarely be identical. You can be physically very aroused without the enjoyment factor being very high, and vice versa. The enjoyment curve can also dip into the negative, if you're frustrated or annoyed or if you have feelings of guilt or shame. For a fulfilling sex life in the long term, it's important for both curves to be as high as possible. This means you'll have a holistic, intense sexual experience.

Exercises

1. Observe yourself during masturbation and sex and answer the questionnaires on pages 33 and 34. Do everything just as usual. If you've never, or only rarely, masturbated, start now and let intuition be your guide. Just do what feels good. It's important to note that though the word *masturbation* technically implies the use of the hand, in this book, masturbation is used to mean any way you pleasure yourself without a partner—by touching yourself in various ways, using a vibrator, squeezing your legs together, etc. The goal of this exercise is to end up with as precise a description as possible—a kind of masturbation log, like the screenplay of a film. Masturbate several times a week: observing yourself might distract you and muddle your normal routine, so it might take some time to get an accurate picture.

2. Figure out how you feel about your sex parts. How much attention do you pay to them in your daily life? How aware are you of your vagina and vulva? When do you think about them? And when you do think about them, are your thoughts positive or negative? Send your sex parts a mental text now and then to ask how they're doing.

Good to know

Why do I have to practice so often? I can't find the time.
If you want to improve your French, you have to practice. If you want to play piano, you have to practice. If you want to learn to dance, same thing. Try to take a little time several times a week—it will add up. Practice several times briefly rather than once for a long time—it's much more effective! Ultimately, it's a simple calculation: you get out what you put in. This applies to sex, too! Your motivation or desire to practice isn't of primary importance—what's important is that you stick to it and incorporate as many short practice sessions into your daily life as possible.

I don't often feel like masturbating. Do I have to force myself?
It's normal that you don't always feel like it. You should never force yourself, and some days your practice simply may not work. Try touching yourself gently, even if you don't orgasm. Most likely, doing this will put you in the mood, but if it's uncomfortable, you can always stop and try again the next day.

Remember, though, that it's important to practice if you want to reach a goal. That sounds worse than it is. Playing scales over and over isn't that much fun, either. But you do it because you know you have to practice if you want to make progress. When, after many, many hours, you can play a piece perfectly because you've practiced it so much, you feel great—and want to play more.

And that's the point: to want more. If you don't see much benefit from what you're doing, you're probably not very motivated to masturbate and have sex. As so often in life, it's a question of cost and benefit. If the benefit increases, we start to like the "cost," or effort more—and it no longer feels so much like effort. To put it simply: the more you practice, the more you'll enjoy it and want to continue over time.

An even simpler trick: the more playfully and inquisitively you approach the exercises, the better it will feel, and the time will fly. Here too: smiling helps!

There are women who have orgasms from penetrative sex just like that. Why is it so different for them? Why don't they have to practice?

That's not exactly true. Even women who have been having orgasms through vaginal penetration since their first time have practiced. They probably just did their training early in life, or without noticing they were doing it. No woman enters the world with her sexual response developed—just like no baby comes out of the womb able to walk. These skills have to be learned. I've observed often in my practice that women who have had orgasms through penetration early in their lives discovered and touched their vaginas at a young age. They too had to practice.

What should I do if I haven't masturbated in ages? What if there's no such thing as "my method"?

Just do what you remember. Do what used to work. Observe yourself as you do it. And if you really don't have a method, that's fine too! Now is the perfect time to develop one. Simply give it a try and find out what feels good! Start by touching in different ways—circling, stroking, pressing, tapping, softer and harder touches—then do more of what you like. Don't pressure yourself to orgasm—just explore.

Why do I have to practice alone? Can't I just make changes directly through sex with my partner?

When you practice alone, you're not distracted and you can do exactly what pleases you. A partner is always also a distraction, a possible source of interruption. When you practice alone, you can direct all your attention to your own sensations. Of course, you can also practice through sex with a partner, if you both concentrate on the sensations of your vagina during foreplay.

At the beginning of my relationship, I came to orgasm much more quickly and more often during sex. Why was that?

Emotional passion, which is usually greater at the beginning of a relationship than later, influences our desire for sex. Hormones massively boost our sensations and cause us to feel touch more intensely. Couples also tend to move much more at the beginning than they do later.

The desire to explore a new body calls for activity. When a relationship is new, we are usually in a phase where everything flows, and time flies. At this stage we're sending and receiving stimulation that leads to greater desire and more orgasms on all levels and through all channels. Some couples look back wistfully at the beginning of their relationship and think they've lost this passion for each other. But this, too, is a fallacy, because passion can also be learned! And you'll learn how later in this book.

CASE STUDY

Lena

LENA IS THIRTY-ONE AND has been in a stable relationship for five years. She's happy in the relationship, loves her boyfriend, and wants to have children with him someday. She doesn't come to see me because of any terrible suffering, and assures me from the beginning that "It's not really even a problem!" But she's worried that it could become one at some point, and wants to keep that from happening, so she made an appointment. Lena tells me that for a while she's been more interested in masturbating than in having sex with her boyfriend. They used to sleep with each other often and take their time about it, but now it only happens twice or three times a month. Usually he starts it. Actually, she'd like to have more sex, she tells me. But she often lacks the time and energy, and in fact the desire, too. It's not tragic: "Other couples have even less sex!" she says, laughing. But she doesn't want sex to become any less frequent than it already is.

We talk about masturbation and sex. Lena tells me that she can come to orgasm quickly and reliably when she does it herself. She lies on her back and presses her clitoris with two fingers. She feels good afterward, but these orgasms aren't earthshaking, either. She only has an orgasm with her boyfriend when he gives her oral sex, and even then, it doesn't always work, and often takes a while. She's never climaxed through penetration. Her boyfriend always has an orgasm during sex. She finds this unfair sometimes, though it seems that this is a common difference between men and women. But it annoys her to have to ask herself if she's doing something wrong, or if something is wrong with her. She's worried that her desire for sex will disappear completely and cause a problem in the relationship.

First I assure her that there's nothing at all wrong with her. Many women feel this way—I've heard similar stories countless times. We talk about the fact that she can change things if she wants to. It requires motivation, time, and patience. Our desire for sex is closely related to how much we're able to enjoy it. If it's only moderately satisfying, we'll only be moderately interested in it.

The insight that she can change something is itself the first step toward this change. Lena thought she needed to learn to accept her situation. I explain to her how she can make the change happen: she'll have to practice the exercises described in this book several times a week for three months. Before our next session, Lena thinks about whether she wants to invest that much time and energy. When she returns, she says she can see that it won't be easy, since she's not good at sticking to things. But she's curious, and wants to give it a try.

Over the next weeks, she comes regularly to me to talk about her discoveries and the next steps. She says that she has a hard time motivating herself, but she likes the fact that the therapy is concrete and simple.

She quickly realizes that something is changing and that her commitment is worth it. She understands her body better, and gets to know it more. She enjoys sex more and more, and she even starts taking the initiative more often herself. Not because she thinks it's time for it, but because she wants to. She says: "Now I have sex for myself, not for the relationship or for my boyfriend."

(Step 3)

WHERE DO I COME FROM?

My Sexual Past

AFTER THE FIRST two steps, it should be fairly clear to you how your arousal works. Perhaps you've realized that what you do alone isn't the same as what you do with your partner. Maybe when you masturbate, you press your legs together, but when you have sex, your legs are spread wide. Maybe you move more when you have sex with a partner than when you're alone. Maybe alone, you always lie on your stomach, but with your partner you're usually on your back. Maybe you like to turn yourself on with porn or erotica, and when you're with another person you miss the visual or mental stimulation. Or you react primarily to slow, gentle touch, but the sex you have with your partner is more on the hard and fast side. When they compare the two kinds of sexual experience, many women realize that during masturbation they mostly touch the clitoris, or a certain part of it, but during sex—during penetration, that is—it's mostly the vagina that gets stimulated. It's easy to see why you wouldn't have an orgasm this way if you don't often touch your vagina when masturbating.

There are several explanations for why women touch themselves more on their external sex parts than internally. For one, the vulva is located outside of the body, so it's simply easier to find and to touch the clitoris—and touching often feels good. It doesn't occur to many girls to actively investigate their vaginas. This is sometimes tied up with shame—female sex parts are still more taboo than their male counterparts. Talking about the female anatomy is delicate and sometimes awkward, and it can be hard to even find the words. Many common terms are either fairly vulgar (like *cunt* or *pussy*) or sound very technical. There's simply no familiar word that refers to the vagina and vulva together. What's more, they're often associated with painful experiences as a teenager or adult: the period flows out through the vagina, tampons are pushed in, at some point it might be beset by a yeast infection, children come into the world through it. Some women might also have sexual traumas that could affect their relationship with their vaginas. You can see how many obstacles there are to developing a positive connection between vagina and brain.

Whether you can come to orgasm through clitoral stimulation doesn't have much to say about whether you can also come to orgasm through stimulation within the vagina. So far, you may only have learned the one way. Just because you can speak French, you can't automatically speak German. The "clitoral" orgasm is therefore not, as is often assumed, the preliminary step to the "vaginal" orgasm. One kind of orgasm is neither the "little sister" of the other kind, nor is it inferior or less valuable. For many, orgasm through clitoral stimulation is simply habit: a wonderful sure thing that can feel good and satisfying.

In order to understand what you've already learned and which synapses have already been formed in your brain, it helps to think back to the past. How was your body treated when you were a child? A teenager? When did you start to masturbate? In order to understand where we are now, we have to understand how we got here.

Try to figure out why you've gotten to know your vagina, or why not. Try to remember whether your first sexual experiences were positive or tied up with feelings of shame.

My history questionnaire

* When did I discover my sex parts?
* How old was I?
* How did my parents and my siblings react?
* As a child, how did I refer to my sex parts?
* How did my parents refer to them?
* When did I first touch my sex parts?
* When was I first aroused?
* What aroused me?
* Where did I touch myself?
* How did I feel when my body changed during puberty?

* When did I first masturbate?
* What was it like?
* What did I do?
* How did I perceive my sex parts?
* When was my first sexual contact with another person?
* How did it feel?
* What did we do?
* What did I like?

IF IT'S HARD to remember, perhaps these statements will help to prompt your thoughts:

My parents called the female sex parts... **Or:** When I was a child, I didn't have a name for my sex parts.

In kindergarten I got caught playing "doctor" with a friend. The teacher was angry and forbade us from doing it again. **Or:** I loved playing doctor.

I found discovering my body exciting. **Or:** I felt shame when I touched myself "down there."

My neighbor, my friend, or my sister showed me how they touched themselves. **Or:** No one showed me how to masturbate.

My friends and I talked a lot about masturbation. **Or:** We didn't talk about masturbation.

I decided to try touching myself because I read about it somewhere. **Or:** It didn't occur to me to touch myself.

I was happy when I got my period. It was a cause for celebration. **Or:** When I first got my period I found it disgusting or embarrassing.

I didn't like it when my body started becoming more womanly. **Or:** I liked it when my body started becoming more womanly.

My first time was painful; it happened against my will. **Or:** I felt almost nothing my first time, and I was disappointed. **Or:** My first time was great.

THINKING BACK WILL help you understand yourself better in the here and now. Many women struggle with their bodies. They blame themselves for not being able to experience their sexuality freely and with pleasure. Don't worry: it's normal for women to have had varied experiences. Some were very curious about their bodies as children, others only became curious later—with their first partners, for example—and still others only wanted to learn more about their bodies and their sexuality as they grew older. Nonetheless, it's common for women to develop a certain *modus vivendi* that they've gotten used to. They use it regularly and it works perfectly. Only years later—perhaps with a new partner or because they've read about it—do they want to change something and expand their repertoire.

Exercises

FROM NOW ON you'll begin slowly expanding on your usual patterns. You might feel like suddenly changing everything at once, but that won't work. As so often in life, you need a bit of time and patience.

Change one detail when you masturbate and observe how it feels. If you usually move your fingers fairly quickly, or use a lot of pressure, try to go slowly and more gently. Or try to change the amount of tension in your body or to vary the tempo.

If you notice that you're no longer feeling much and your arousal is diminishing, return to your trusty old ways. Let your arousal grow, and then start again with the new version, with the changed rhythms. It's important to not suddenly change your whole technique, but rather change just one element of it. Otherwise you might completely lose your arousal. Repeat the exercise several times a week. It doesn't matter whether you ultimately come this way or not.

Good to know

I find thinking about my childhood sexuality uncomfortable. Why is that?

When we think about our young selves (or even our own children) in relationship to sex, we see ourselves or them with grown-up eyes. But a child doesn't see her sexual development or the discovery of her body from this perspective. Children discover themselves and their environment with pleasure. They want to find out what it looks like inside their mouths, and how their nostrils feel. They touch themselves and look at themselves. They want to investigate their bodies, including their sex parts. As adults, we see this in a different context, and understand it as embarrassing or dangerous. But it's our adult self that judges this way. As children, we thought differently. A child likes it when she has pleasant sensations, and she tries to repeat them. But she notices when adults react strangely to her behavior, and begins to find it strange herself.

Is it normal for children to play doctor?

Yes! It helps them explore what their bodies are like and indulge their curiosity. This is a very natural part of discovering their bodies. As long as the children are close in age and one isn't pressuring the other, it's nothing at all to worry about.

Why exactly should I change individual elements of my process when I masturbate? What I've always done works perfectly.

Like other women, you have developed a specific pattern of arousal over the years. So why develop an alternative pattern? Well, the more different patterns you have, the more different kinds of touch you can react to and enjoy. For example: A woman always rubs her clitoris clockwise. When her partner tries to pleasure her, he or she often goes in the wrong direction, or uses too much pressure, or goes too slowly. She can sense that it won't work this way and tries with all her might to induce a feeling of arousal. If she weren't dependent on her very specific pattern, but rather had a wider repertoire, it would be easier for her to have more fun during sex. Her partner wouldn't have to do exactly what she was used to; instead, she could let herself be surprised and thereby increase her arousal. Of course, a woman can and should tell her partner exactly what arouses her and what he or she should do. But the sex will be more varied and fun if she doesn't have to follow a special program but instead can try out lots of different things and find many of them arousing.

This goes for men too, by the way! Many men react primarily to arousal techniques that they use on themselves, and they want women to touch them the same way. They can only increase their arousal when they feel exactly the same pressure they use when masturbating. You'll read about how a man can break out of his pattern and expand his repertoire later, in the chapter for men.

Can I use a vibrator for the exercises? I always use one when I masturbate.

Using a vibrator is an efficient method for quickly triggering and increasing arousal. But penises can't vibrate. So if you only come to orgasm with a vibrator, it's understandable that a penis doesn't do much for you. If you want to come to orgasm through your partner's body, you should learn to come without a vibrator. But don't just put your vibrator away—that will quickly lead to frustration. Keep using it, but now and then, turn it down to a slower vibration. Or use your fingers in between, and if your arousal starts to subside, pick up your vibrator again.

Martina

MARTINA HAS TWO TEENAGE children and has been happily married for twenty-five years. She comes to see me because her "clitoris has stopped working." She tells me that she's always been able to come through masturbation, but since menopause it's no longer always so easy. Sometimes she even has pain after her orgasm. She has regular sex with her husband, "every two weeks or so," but she doesn't find it particularly arousing. She goes just along with it "because it's part of the deal, and he likes it so much."

I ask about her childhood. She answers quickly that she never had any problems—she had great parents and never experienced any trauma. Martina is the oldest of four children and her parents were very loving. Sex was never discussed. She doesn't remember whether she ever played doctor. There's only one thing she remembers: Once when she was "playing" with one of the girls next door, the girl's mother caught them and told them that what they were doing was disgusting. Martina tells me that she realized quite early that it felt good when she lay on her teddy bear and pressed its nose between her legs. She liked that and did it often.

Then we talk about the development of her body. When she reached puberty, her body became more womanly. Even today she's fairly unhappy with her curves. After she had children she became even curvier. She remembers that she got her period at fourteen and at first thought she must be sick. Her mother had hugged her and said: "Poor thing, now it's happening to you too." At first, she'd worn pads, but she found them very uncomfortable. Later she switched to tampons, which weren't so bad.

I tell her that it's important to think about whether she can develop a good relationship to her body and her sex parts. Martina's development is typical. Some women struggle with their bodies. Some of them were never able to develop a positive, sensual relationship with themselves. This is a shame, because if you have a loving relationship with your sex parts and your body, you'll feel more during sex. For that to happen, you have to learn to understand your body better.

I also explain to her that it's normal for her sex parts to change during menopause. In order to keep up with the changes in our bodies, we usually have to adjust our arousal patterns—otherwise we'll lose the desire for sex and might even feel pain. Martina has always aroused herself primarily through pressure and tension, as she "practiced" with her teddy bear. The arousal pattern that she developed as a child hasn't changed. But her friction receptors are no longer so sensitive, and she tenses her muscles more and more. That's why Martina now has the feeling that "her clitoris has stopped working right." But Martina can also practice and expand her patterns, if she wants to experience a new kind of arousal and pleasure.

(Step 4)

MOVE IT!

Why Movement Matters

B EFORE WE CONTINUE, let's take stock. What have we learned in the first three steps?

* It's important to know the anatomy of the vulva and vagina.
* Arousal and enjoyment are not the same.
* Like the clitoris, the vagina can also be a source of arousal and enjoyment.

* But: it can't feel much if it hasn't been touched and sensitized.
* If it's touched more often, it will feel more.
* If it feels more, the possibilities for arousal and pleasure grow.
* Our sexual past has a big impact on our current sex lives.
* The clitoris is much bigger than we thought.
* The vulva, too, needs care.
* There's a lot to gain when we have multiple different arousal patterns at our disposal instead of just one.

AND NOW IT'S time to bring movement into the mix! Many women are relatively passive during penetrative sex. They might be active lovers before and after, working hard to give their partners pleasure and moving a lot—but during penetration their bodies are stiff and tense. What about you? Think back to the questionnaires from Step 2. Are you one of these women? Do you move a lot during sex and while masturbating? Are your muscles tense or relaxed? Is your breathing deep or shallow? Are your legs slack or cramped?

Some women tense their bodies to increase their arousal, but it would really help them to move more during sex and masturbation. The reason once more lies in biology: Our autonomic nervous system works around the clock, automatically controlling all of our body's necessary functions and taking care of things we can't voluntarily influence, like respiration, digestion, and metabolism. It contains two complementary substructures: the sympathetic nervous system primarily sends signals that facilitate action, while the parasympathetic sends signals that facilitate recovery.

When primarily the sympathetic nervous system is active, we're in "fight-or-flight" mode: the whole body is on alert. A large quantity of adrenaline is released. You sweat, become focused, breathe shallowly, and your heart beats quickly. Your muscles are tensed. Digestion is paralyzed—which makes sense, since you wouldn't want to have to run to the bathroom in the middle of a fight. Thoughts circle, and emotions during fight-or-flight are on the negative side: you feel fear, anger, and hatred. The other is your enemy.

When primarily the parasympathetic nervous system is active, our bodies are in a stable "relaxation" mode: we're calm, with a slow pulse and deep breaths. The body can attend to digestion and recuperation. Your thoughts aren't purposeful, but rather creative and associative. Your emotions are positive; you feel joy and love. The other is your friend.

Many people's bodies are often in fight-or-flight mode. They want to achieve something, and they fight for it. They're stressed at work, their muscles are cramped, digestion goes on strike, they hardly take time for lunch, their days are jam-packed. They're efficient. Many of us are used to this state, and it's become our norm. For our bodies, however, it represents a dangerous state of permanent strain, which can lead to physical and/or psychological problems. In relaxation mode, on the other hand, we have original ideas and are creative. We enjoy the moment; we're completely in the here and now. We really ought to spend more time in this mode than in fight-or-flight mode: it's like a filling station for body and soul.

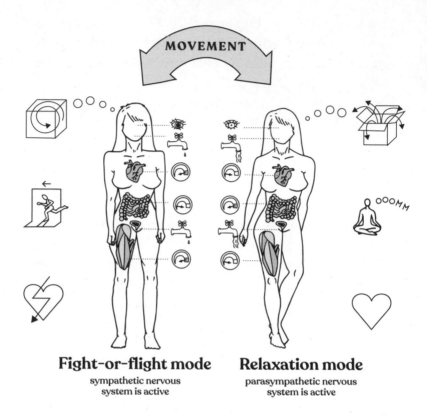

Fight-or-flight mode
sympathetic nervous
system is active

Relaxation mode
parasympathetic nervous
system is active

WHAT DOES THIS mean for our sex lives? Some women tense their muscles (including those of the pelvic floor) during sex and move little. Maybe they're absorbing their partner's hard thrusts, maybe they're trying to hold on to their arousal, or maybe they think that it feels better and tighter for a man this way. This tension puts the body in fight-or-flight mode. Emotions pull predominantly toward defense: a person who's tense tends to feel fear, anger, disgust, and shame. A woman in fight-or-flight mode sees herself and her partner through more critical eyes and may start to brood. Her partner seems like the enemy and easily annoys her. Many women know these feelings but don't understand where they come from—and so they feel bad about them. This can lead to a jumble of emotions: they know they like their partner, but somehow they get exasperated with him or her in the context of their shared sexuality.

In addition, we've already briefly mentioned that it's easy to be distracted in fight-or-flight mode. Since in this mode, you are highly aware of your environment—ultimately, you have to be able to ascertain whether there's a threat and where it's coming from—even the smallest change during sex can cause you to lose your desire. Your partner suddenly changes his tempo, for example, and instantaneously your arousal falls apart. The same thing happens when he changes position or you hear a loud noise. In fight-or-flight mode, it's also more likely for your arousal and fantasies to be disturbed by thoughts of your last credit card bill.

But arousal does require tension as well. In relaxation mode we enjoy sex—we're completely relaxed and not so easily distracted. The curve of enjoyment is very high: we take pleasure in our partner and feel much love and affection—but we lack the tension that's needed for arousal. In this state, orgasm is practically impossible. The "threshold" that would allow us to not only enjoy sex to the fullest but also be fully aroused and reach climax can't be crossed.

There's only one way to succeed in this balancing act: with movement—which means tension and relaxation at the same time. When you move your body, certain muscles work hard, while their counterparts relax. This puts you both in fight-or-flight mode (important for arousal)—and in relaxation mode (important for pleasure).

Why movement is so important

* Parts of the body that are moved get more blood flow. This makes them more sensitive. Touch feels more pleasant. In sex this means: when you move your pelvis, your vagina can feel more.

* When your vagina is well supplied with blood, it grows moist and expands, allowing more space for a penis or fingers. If you tend to have pain from sex, movement can dramatically reduce it or fix the problem altogether.

* To feel good, you have to relax. When you're tense, you may have negative feelings and start to worry. When you move during sex, you'll quiet these thoughts and be able to feel more intense affection for your partner.

* When you move your body, you're more in touch with it. You won't feel your arousal in just one place but will be able to sense it flowing through your whole body. Movement helps distribute the arousal. Your orgasm, too, won't feel so much like it's just in one place; it will be in your whole body.

* When you feel your vagina more, you want sex more. Why? It's simple: You feel much more and it feels better to you. And anything that feels good is something we have a desire to experience more often.

THE BIG QUESTION remains: What's the best way to move during masturbation or sex with a partner? The answer is: However you like! Swing yourself back and forth, move your pelvis in circles, stretch out, change positions, and vary the tempo—sometimes gentle, sometimes more intense. The more you experiment when masturbating and having sex, the more clearly you'll see which movements you like. This can take some time, especially when you haven't moved much before. Don't worry: it's not about starting to dance wildly in bed all of a sudden. It's enough to make micromovements—start with minimal movements and expand your range of motion as you practice over the course of a week. And by the way: breathing is a movement too. The deeper you breathe, the stronger your internal movement.

Movement is one of the most important factors for a satisfying orgasm and for fulfilling, holistic sex. But there's one thing to know: starting to move more might temporarily turn your sex life upside down. It's not like a switch that you can flick, and *boom*—you enjoy sex more and hop from one climax to the next. When you start to move, it might initially be suboptimal for your arousal. Perhaps you're quite simply not used to so much action, but rather to tension and little movement—if this is the pattern you've mentally saved in connection with your arousal. With time you'll feel more, and you'll notice that your arousal and enjoyment reach a whole new level. You'll only know how great your sexual potential is when you see the difference.

But at first, it can be frustrating when you start to move more. Ultimately, you're turning a well-rehearsed system upside down. You're trying to teach your body to produce desire and arousal on its own. The goal is to be your own biggest source of arousal. Obviously, that won't happen overnight. But it can be done! As I said in the introduction, sex works just like many other things. It too is a matter of practice.

Think of a sport you like. Swimming, perhaps? When you first started, you might not have been keen on it. You weren't in shape, and you were totally exhausted after ten minutes. Your muscles were sore; your body hurt. It was taxing. Maybe you stopped then and there. Or maybe you stuck to it. And at some point you were in better shape, and it started to go better. Swimming became easy. And later, it was even pleasant, and you looked forward to it. Because you began to feel good during your swims as well as afterward. And at some point, you started to really miss it if you couldn't swim for a few days. Because now it seemed to work automatically, and it was tons of fun. But you had to get through the awkward times at the beginning first. It's like that with sex too. If you want to get the exhilaration, the maximum pleasure, the maximum arousal, you have to accept that a few rounds might be rough and clumsy at the beginning. But it's worth it!

Exercises

1. Start moving when you masturbate, using small movements at first. Circle your hips. Swing your pelvis back and forth. Try to not just lie there. Consciously tense your muscles and then relax them. When your arousal

diminishes—as it probably will—return to your reliable pattern and use it to increase your arousal. Then start moving again—again, only a little at first. With time you'll notice that your arousal lasts longer and you feel more and more. If you don't come to orgasm, it's okay. Repeat this exercise several times a week.

2. Touch your vagina inch by inch, and consciously observe how it feels in different places. Create an internal map of your vagina. How does it feel right at the front? How about an inch farther in on the left side? What does the "G-zone" on the front wall feel like?

   As you go about your day, try to be more conscious of your vagina. You've touched your vulva and vagina many times now, so you know how they feel. You know how they're built. Now begin trying to be aware of your sex parts in your daily life. Walk so that you feel your vagina. Repeatedly tense and release the muscles of your pelvic floor. Breathe deep into your abdomen. Try to consciously perceive your vagina. And—even more important!—try to develop a sense of pride in it.

3. Imagine there's a clock face at the entrance to your vagina. Determine where 12, 3, 6, and 9 o'clock are. Now touch the entrance to your vagina with one or two fingers. How does each specific spot feel? Now imagine the clock face is deeper in your vagina. Touch the four spots again, now farther inside. How do each of these places feel? Do you feel differences? Where are you sensitive, and where are you less sensitive?

This is a good exercise to involve your partner in: How precisely do you feel which spot he or she is touching? What changes when he or she touches different spots? And what difference does it make when it's not your finger that you feel, but your partner's?

Good to know

I hardly feel anything when I touch my vagina. What am I doing wrong?

You might think you feel nothing—but it's never nothing. Sensation is a spectrum: at first you might hardly feel anything, then you feel that your finger is inside your vagina, then you can tell whether it feels pleasant or unpleasant, then it might feel pleasant, later slightly arousing, and much later very arousing. At first, it's a problem of expectations and perception. If you expect vaginal stimulation to be very arousing from the beginning, you'll be frustrated. But when you're curious and open and simply accept what you feel, you'll notice the changes and celebrate them.

What's important to know is that arousal is triggered by a reflex when certain conditions are met. It's comparable to any other reflex in your body. For example, the reflex in your knee: when a certain spot is hit, your lower leg kicks out. You can't intentionally provoke this—it happens when the necessary conditions in the body (blow to the knee) are met. The arousal reflex functions similarly to your leg kicking. If it's triggered, arousal begins and can be increased to the point of orgasm. Orgasm too is a reflex that can be triggered. It can't be deliberately produced, but we can do things to create the necessary conditions, namely: produce arousal, distribute it widely through the body, and finally channel it to a climax.

Stimulation of the vagina feels very different than stimulation of the clitoris. Why is this?

Every woman feels clitoral arousal differently. Many describe it as "sharper." It's more central. Vaginal arousal is softer and bigger. Often women actually do feel this vague, soft arousal, but they don't know how to classify it, and don't associate the feeling with arousal. This can be learned. It's important to learn to be open to new sensations and perceptions.

In my practice, I often hear women say that they don't feel what they were expecting. When I ask for details, however, they've clearly felt arousal. We have to bear in mind that expectations are concrete ideas. When we expect a very specific reaction from our body, we miss the reactions that we didn't anticipate.

Can I have an orgasm through penetration if I don't move?

Of course. You can come to orgasm with a quickie and lots of tension if, for example, your cervix is well sensitized and is stimulated through penetration. The goal is to be able to feel lots of arousal and satisfaction with various kinds of sex, whether short or long, quick or slow.

What about Fifty Shades of Grey? *He does all the work and she just lies there and has multiple orgasms. I know it's just a story, but it inspired millions of women. Many women find not being able to move arousing, right?*

It's great when couples arouse each other this way—it can be an exciting way to play. In this case, the arousal is physically "logical." When you're tied up, your senses are heightened because you're excited. The tension makes your sensations more intense. It's understandable if this brings you to orgasm. But if a woman were to always and exclusively have sex this way—three times a week she gets tied to the bedposts—at some point the likelihood that she'll come will also diminish. Because her arousal is based on excitement, and the kick lessens every time, because she gets used to it. Couples who have sex this way have to be very inventive and use sophisticated techniques to keep the effect the same.

Sina

SINA, TWENTY-SEVEN YEARS OLD, comes to me because she finds her own behavior during sex confusing. She's been with her boyfriend for a year, sleeps with him often, and it's wonderful. At least usually. She tells me that sometimes he annoys her while they're at it. And that now and then she even has to stop the sex for this reason. She finds this unsettling. Her rebuffs unsettle him too, which makes her feel terrible. Sina simply can't explain where her annoyance comes from.

I ask her how they have sex. What do they do, exactly? What happens when? Sina tells me that she knows exactly where she likes to be touched. And sometimes he picks up on this and does everything right. Then it's great. But sometimes he just touches the wrong place. And it annoys her because she feels like she's told him often enough. But most of all she's annoyed by her own annoyance. That she can't just let go and enjoy herself. Sometimes she really gets caught up in his "failure."

It's important for Sina to understand that her annoyance starts long before they stop having sex. She's waiting to see if her boyfriend does it "right," testing him, in a way, and then she gets angry when he doesn't succeed. During sex she doesn't tell him what she likes. They talk *about* sex, but not *during* sex. She doesn't ask him to please touch her half an inch to the left. She thinks that would be superfluous. She explains: "I moaned when he did it right, that should be enough!" I ask if she thinks he's intentionally touching her "wrong." She denies this vehemently.

I explain that she can either give her boyfriend clear instructions or take matters into her own hands and stimulate herself where she likes. There's also a third option: She can develop her sexuality step-by-step to the point that she's no longer so dependent on him doing something precisely "correctly." If she feels more and her sex parts are well sensitized, it won't matter so much if his fingers are a bit too far to the left.

Sina decides to follow this last option, and by practicing the exercises in the book, she learns to expand her patterns of arousal and feel pleasure from different kinds of movement and touch. Now during sex with her boyfriend, she is able to relax and enjoy herself without worrying about things going "wrong."

(Step 5)

THE PELVIC FLOOR

Why It's
So Important

Y OU MAY ALREADY have heard that the famous, much-discussed pelvic floor is important for arousal and the ability to orgasm. And you might even have read somewhere that it's good to strengthen it: there's pelvic floor gymnastics, pelvic floor training with balls or dildos, and even pelvic floor yoga. When a woman tenses her pelvic floor, it's said, she'll feel more during sex. And for some men it's a nice experience when the vagina feels narrower. (The reason, by the way, is that it feels more like a hand surrounding the penis—like masturbation.) Everywhere we see tips and tricks in magazines for how we can learn to tense the pelvic floor with more control. Many are familiar with this tension from yoga or Pilates. But in my experience, it's just as important to be able to relax these muscles. More precisely, playing with the muscles, tensing and releasing them, is decisive for arousal and orgasm!

But let's get to know this famous pelvic floor better first. It consists of a complex network of muscles and connective tissue that surround the vagina and urethra, the rectum, and the anus. Therefore, the muscles of the pelvic floor encompass parts of the body that are central to sex. When you tense and release them, you can help increase your arousal. Playing with tensing and releasing also increases circulation, and therefore the sensitivity in the pelvis. And it ensures that the vagina becomes moister during sex.

When the muscles are very tense, the vulva and vagina receive less blood flow. And parts of the body that receive less blood flow eventually become less sensitive. Tension also makes the vagina drier and more narrow. For this reason, some women have pain during sex. In addition, tension is associated with stress. And stress doesn't really go very well with feelings of love and desire.

But arousal also doesn't work without tension. That's the arousal paradox: with too much or too little tension, it can't function. The pelvic muscles tense automatically during arousal. This is important, because a woman can't come to orgasm with completely relaxed muscles. Her arousal would just fall asleep, so to speak. On the other hand, sometimes the pelvic floor is almost continuously tense during sex—this happens above all with young women. And muscles that are always tensed eventually grow numb.

How can you tell whether your pelvic floor is tense or relaxed in a resting state? Try the following test: sit on a chair with your back straight and your feet on the floor. Tense the muscles of your pelvic floor as if you're trying to stop yourself from peeing. Now imagine your pelvic floor is an elevator: as you tense more and more, the muscles rise higher and higher. Go up to the second floor, then up to the third and fourth. Wait at the top and count to ten slowly. Then—this is important—go down again: third floor, second floor, ground floor.

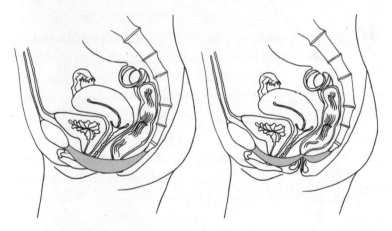

The pelvic floor, relaxed   *The pelvic floor, tensed*

Which was easier? Going up or going down? Some young women find the pulling up noticeably easier than the slowly going down. They're better able to tense than to release.

So how do you learn to relax your pelvic floor so that it can receive more blood flow and heighten your arousal during sex? The following exercises are the answer.

Exercises

1. Elevator: Do the exercise as described above but con-
    centrate on the "descent." Try to really let go at the
    end—it should feel as if you're about to pee your pants.

2. Several times a day, tense the muscles of your pelvic
    floor for three seconds, and then slowly release them.
    After the intense contraction, the relaxation will be
    deeper. This is therefore a reliable way to get your pel-
    vic muscles to relax.

3. Practice breathing into your belly. Place your hand on
    your belly and wait until it curves when you breathe in.
    Now try to breathe more deeply with each breath. Let
    your belly grow big like a balloon, then let it contract,
    and blow it up again.

4. Put your hand on your vulva and try to feel your
    breathing there. What do your fingers feel when you
    breathe in and out deeply?

5. If you're already easily able to tense and release the
    muscles of your pelvic floor, you can try playing with
    the individual muscles. Tense first your left butt cheek,
    then your right. Now tense the muscles around your
    anus, and then the muscles farther forward, by your
    vagina and urethra. Then try to release the muscles of
    your anus while keeping the front ones tensed. You'll
    never be able to control these muscles in a completely
    separate way, because they're complexly intertwined.

But the better you learn to control them, the more specifically they can transport your arousal.

Good to know

Why do I have to be able to perceive the muscles of the pelvic floor so precisely?

Some women understand their vaginas as passive. When you can sense the muscles more specifically, the vagina becomes an active body part. By playing with the pelvic floor muscles, and because your vagina is becoming more sensitive through increased touch, you'll have more desire to actively take something into your vagina.

How can I tell if the muscles of my pelvic floor are strong and well trained?

Place your finger in your vagina and tense your pelvic floor. If your vagina doesn't get narrower, you're either tensing your stomach or your buttocks, or your pelvic floor muscles really aren't in shape. Then only one thing will help: practice, practice, practice. If you want to know for sure, you can go to a pelvic floor physical therapist—which I highly recommend. Many women regularly do Pilates or yoga, but they do the pelvic floor exercises wrong without realizing it. Then it's likely to be hard to implement the exercises in this book.

I've had kids. Do I really need to learn to relax my pelvic floor?

If you've given birth at least once, you'll probably have to practice not only relaxing but also contracting. Women experience and describe the physical changes after giving birth differently. Some describe a feeling of pressure. Others say their pelvic floor muscles feel numb, or that it feels "open down there." Others talk about pain in the perineum and the feeling that the uterus is "slipping down." After childbirth, the pelvic floor needs relief, stimulation, and training in order to stabilize. Do the elevator exercise, but concentrate on the ascent. You can also train your pelvic floor muscles by tensing them several times a day, as if you want to hold back a stream of urine. But be careful: don't do this exercise if you really have to go to the bathroom, as that can be bad for the bladder. Tense your pelvic floor muscles really tightly for three seconds, then slowly release them. Make sure that you're not tensing your buttocks and your legs, but rather your internal muscles. And take time with the exercise: if you do it slowly, you'll feel more.

When I want to bring myself to orgasm, my muscles are totally tensed. Is that bad?

Many women tense their muscles when they want to come to orgasm. This helps them to channel the arousal they've built up and to trigger the orgasm reflex. Maybe you already noticed this when you did the masturbation questionnaire in Step 2. The tension builds, is at its highest point right before orgasm, and then explodes and releases. This is great, and works very well all by itself. A woman can come quickly to orgasm this way and enjoy the relaxation afterward.

But in sex with a partner, this can cause two problems: First of all, when we're tense, we're more easily distracted.

Anything that disturbs the tension annoys us. Therefore, your partner can become a distracting factor. Second, some women aren't able to tense their vaginas when there's a penis inside. As a result, it's hard or even impossible to reach orgasm, because the woman is unable to achieve the tension she needs. With this too it's all a matter of balance. You need some tension to go over the edge, but when you've gotten used to a lot of tension over a long period of time, it can lead to the difficulties mentioned above.

Claudia and Monica

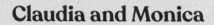

CLAUDIA AND MONICA, both thirty-eight, have been friends since elementary school, and come to see me because they want to enjoy sex with their partners more again after childbirth. Claudia has two daughters and Monica has a little boy. The two women couldn't be more different: Claudia is a *bon vivant*—she stresses that she rarely exercises; nonetheless, she's very slim. Since giving birth to her first child, she's tried to strengthen her pelvic floor. She's read that it's important. Still, she's not terribly disciplined: when she thinks of it, maybe while she's waiting for the bus, she does an exercise she once read about. But she seldom thinks of it. Monica, on the other hand, goes to Pilates twice a week and also does pelvic floor exercises at home several times a week. She's very disciplined and in shape.

Claudia feels very little during sex and blames giving birth and what she calls her "worn out" pelvic floor. Monica feels much more during sex, at least at first, but the longer it lasts, the less she feels. She's annoyed and doesn't understand why she feels so little despite the fact that she's trained her pelvic floor so well and tenses it so much during sex.

I give them the following homework assignment: to insert a finger in the entrance to their vaginas and then tense the pelvic floor. A week later, they report on their findings: Claudia says she tensed her pelvic floor just like she did when she did the exercises at the bus station, but her finger didn't feel any change. Monica says that the walls of her vagina were hard as a rock before she even started tensing.

I show Claudia exercises for the pelvic floor that teach her how to tense the right muscles and how to train purposefully and selectively. Monica, on the other hand, realizes how tense she always is, and that she has to learn to relax the muscles of her pelvic floor. When they're constantly tense, they receive little blood flow and will eventually start to become numb. That's why Monica starts to feel less the longer sex goes on.

For homework, I give them five exercises that will teach them to perceive the muscles of their pelvic floor better. They notice the first changes quickly. Claudia's finger starts to feel more and more when she tenses her muscles in the exercises—natural biofeedback. In general, she perceives more in her vagina, even when she's not tensing. She says her sex parts have "woken up." She feels more feminine and describes her sex parts as lively and active, and she has more desire for sex with her partner.

Monica does the exercises as well, concentrating more on releasing her muscles. Since she now more consciously feels when she's tensing her muscles, she's also better able to regulate the tension. She can now purposefully tense and release her pelvic floor, and through this play, she feels more during sex.

(Step 6)

ALL IN YOUR HEAD?

Sexual Fantasies

W E'VE CONCENTRATED PRIMARILY on the body so far, but it's now time to turn our attention to the mind. Sexual fantasies are wonderful! Isn't it amazing to see what kinds of erotic films our own brains produce, and how arousing we can find our own thoughts?

These fantasies don't necessarily give us much information about what we actually want to experience in the real world, however. A woman who turns herself on with fantasies of being forcefully seduced doesn't really want to be raped. A woman who fantasizes about sex with another woman might not necessarily want to act on it. Sexual fantasies don't have to have anything to do with our actual sexual preferences. Only rarely do they betray repressed desires. This is important to realize, because many women are ashamed of their fantasies or even disgusted by them.

Of course, there is a connection between a person's sexual fantasies and the way they become aroused. The way you use your body during sex is translated in your sexual fantasies: If you massage the inside of your vagina when you masturbate, you'll likely start to fantasize about taking something—a penis, a dildo, or fingers—into your vagina. A woman who's very tense when she masturbates and primarily brings herself to orgasm through friction and pressure is probably also quite tense in her fantasies. She may think of something powerful, dangerous, or strong: to be taken roughly, for example, tied to the bed, or whipped. The more the vagina feels, the bigger a role it's likely to play in fantasies. I've noticed that when women start to discover their own vaginas, they often fantasize about other women for a while—even if they're normally not attracted to women. This makes total sense, since they're beginning to eroticize their own female sex parts.

But again: fantasies are fantasies are fantasies. No more and no less. They're great and important because they're a source of arousal. Some women need fantasies or some kind of gateway arousal before they start to want sex. They wait for a signal from their bodies, a demand for satisfaction. They wait until they receive this request. Many women are convinced that their appetite doesn't come through eating—through sex, that is—but rather has to be there first. Some know how to intentionally trigger this arousal reflex by thinking back to a situation they've experienced, or watching some porn they like. Many more women have no idea what their "fuse" is—how they can induce arousal. They think arousal is a matter of chance.

Another common experience is when the arousal reflex is in fact triggered, but the woman doesn't notice it. In the next steps, the goal is to be more conscious of the reflex and, above all, focusing not too much on the chance presence of initial arousal but rather on our sensations themselves. This way you can learn to better perceive the reflex and exert more influence over it. Our next goal is therefore to turn our concentration toward our own sensations during sex. When we do this, a gateway arousal is no longer necessary for us to be open to sex.

Exercises

1. Start to write down your sexual fantasies and notice whether they transform over time. When you change the way you stimulate yourself, your fantasies will also change. If you find writing down your fantasies uncomfortable, just note down keywords. If that's hard too, observe yourself the next time you masturbate. What are you thinking about, what arouses you, what do you think about right before orgasm? Do you enjoy your fantasies or are you ashamed of them? A few weeks later, observe yourself again. Has anything changed in your mental movie?

Fantasy questionnaire:

* In your fantasies, are you a woman or a man?
* Are you active?
* Are you a part of the scenario?
* Do you watch?
* Who else is involved?

2. Change another detail when you masturbate and notice how it feels. Instead of changing your rhythm or pressure, for example, change your position. If you usually lie on your back, turn over onto your stomach. Or stand. Or sit. If your arousal subsides, return to your usual position. Repeat the exercise several times a week.

Good to know

As soon as I change something when I masturbate, whether it's pressure, rhythm, or simply position, my arousal disappears. And it doesn't come back right away when I return to my normal techniques. Sometimes it takes three times as long before I come. Sometimes I don't come at all. What's wrong with me?

This reaction is totally normal. Every woman who wants to make a change gets frustrated at some point and maybe even wants to give up. Some women even think for a while that they've lost their ability to orgasm. Don't worry: your orgasm isn't lost. It's just tied to a specific pattern, to a clear sequence of touch, a particular spot on your vulva, or to pressure and tension. The slightest deviation can completely put you off your stride. An example:

As a child I studied guitar and had terrible finger position. I neither wanted to nor was able to change it, no matter how often my teacher pointed it out. I didn't see the point: everything was working fine. At some point my teacher said: "If you want to make progress, you have to change your finger position." The way I was doing it, I could play passably well, but if I tried to play faster or do something more complex, I hit a wall. I changed my finger position and . . . couldn't play at all anymore. It just didn't work. I was so frustrated—my technique was taken away from me. I couldn't play with the new "correct" technique. It was as if all the time I'd spent practicing over the years had been for naught. I had to invest a lot of work and motivation into learning to play again. But in the end, it was worth it. I got better and better and playing brought me more and more pleasure, and practicing got easier. At some point it didn't even feel like practicing anymore—I looked forward to it!

Your frustration is normal, and can often come with a change of technique. But don't let it grow so much that you never want to play again! Whenever you get annoyed, return to your old technique. Now and then, do it just like you've always done it. There's nothing wrong with that. It's good for you to feel good, and to see how great your abilities already are. It also doesn't matter if you don't come to orgasm when you're practicing a new technique. You're learning, all the same. Of course, a pleasant experience will help your motivation—and as a side note: whatever you do, if you smile while you're doing it, you'll have a nicer experience.

You can change a detail, continue for a few minutes, and note what happens to your arousal. If it drops, you can always go back to your old routine and continue the way you know how. It's completely normal for you not to be immediately aroused when you stimulate a spot that's not used to being touched.

I usually watch porn when I masturbate. Is that still okay?

Porn can be a source of arousal. If it's your main source, things will get difficult, since when you watch porn, your focus is outside your body, and you won't be able to pay as much attention to what's happening inside you and how your arousal develops. When you have sex with your partner without watching porn, it might start to get harder for you to become and stay aroused. But porn can be a helpful source of arousal, and it's completely fine to watch it if it's something you enjoy. Ideally, you have various sources of arousal. Going without porn on occasion might help you develop different sources.

If you want, you can also change your porn consumption step-by-step. First step: now and then, close your eyes. Second step: turn the screen away for increasing periods of time. Third step: just listen and concentrate increasingly on your body and your sensations.

I don't watch porn, but I like to read erotica when I want to get in the mood. Can I keep doing that?

Reading involves your brain more, since it requires you to use your imagination. What happens in your sex parts is therefore a kind of echo of what happens in your head. If you want to be aroused by touching your vulva and vagina, erotica will distract you. Try starting without reading, and only pick up your book if you feel like you're going to lose your arousal, or if you can't induce it after a long time (up to twenty minutes). Or read to turn yourself on, but then put your book away and concentrate more on your sensations. If your arousal falls apart completely, pick up the book again.

I don't read erotica or watch porn, I just use my fantasies to get aroused. That's okay, right?

Sexual fantasies are a great source of arousal, and they can be very enriching. Most people have fantasies. But if you notice that you can only increase your arousal with certain fantasies, and that your arousal is easily disturbed— for example when your partner makes the "wrong" movement—things can get complicated. Because this means that your arousal is dependent on following a specific fantasy.

If you want to widen your repertoire, it's important for your vagina and vulva to be part of the process of increasing your arousal. If your focus is on a fantasy, your arousal will disappear if you get distracted. Staying in your fantasy during sex with a partner can prove to be difficult, not to mention a bit unromantic.

For many women, sexual fantasies stop working as soon as another person is involved. Maybe when they masturbate they're tense, and have hard fantasies of being dominated. But when they move during sex with their partner, they're not tense, and it's hard to concentrate on the fantasy. As a result, the arousal diminishes and it's hard to reach orgasm. The goal isn't to change the fantasy but rather to alter the understanding that the fantasy is necessary for arousal.

How can this be done? Certainly not by trying to force yourself not to think about your fantasy anymore. Fantasies arise from the way you're aroused: whether you move or are tense, and so on. If you want to change them, you'll also have to adapt your arousal patterns. Nonetheless, fantasies are and remain an important source of arousal that you should definitely make use of.

What happens when my thoughts keep circling and I just can't turn them off?

First of all: don't worry! This happens to many women. Stress at work, a fight with your partner, the fact that there are still dirty dishes in the sink . . . emotions and thoughts naturally mirror the body; the more tense your body is, the more your thoughts will circle. This has already been thoroughly discussed in Step 4. Try to move your body. Breathe out slowly (important!) and try to concentrate on your body. Feel the sensations deep within. If it's hard for you to focus on your sex parts, just concentrate on your finger. The more complex your movements are, the harder it will be for you to think about other things. Of course, there will be days when you simply can't turn your mind off—you don't have to force anything. If that's the case: just rest your hand on your vulva and give it warmth and love.

Julia

JULIA IS A SMART, attractive business executive. She's forty-one, has no children, and is in a healthy, happy relationship. She comes to me because she's annoyed and confused by her fantasies. She says she's never talked to anyone about this problem. She didn't dare, because she found it too embarrassing. It takes her a while to begin to tell me about them.

When Julia wants to arouse herself, she imagines standing on a stage, naked from the waist down, with everyone staring at her. For her to come to orgasm, the fantasy gets "even more brutal." Julia imagines herself in a gang bang with many men. She's held down, can't move, and is "fucked in every hole." She's very confused that this arouses her. She doesn't really want to experience such a thing. Julia says she's very liberated and anything but submissive. She wants to know what this fantasy means and whether she should experiment with a gang bang in reality. She's afraid that her fantasy is a repressed desire—which to her is a terrible thought. Therefore, she often feels guilty after masturbating. She's disgusted by herself and feels bad, but other fantasies don't arouse her. She's also tried porn, but she's noticed that her body only reacts to the same kind of intense scenes she fantasizes about.

Julia uses these fantasies when she wants to come to orgasm with her boyfriend as well. But then it's more difficult to hold on to them, because her boyfriend distracts her. And when he's there, she feels even worse about the "intense scenes," and it almost feels to her like she's cheating on him. She usually doesn't think about her fantasies when she's with her partner, therefore, and just enjoys the sex with him, though she knows that she probably won't come to orgasm.

The first thing I say to her is: "Thoughts are free. Fantasies are fantasies." What she experiences and thinks is completely normal, and her fantasy is actually a common one. This doesn't mean that Julia has to realize the fantasy, or that she has a hidden desire to be held down and dominated. She should allow herself to simply accept these fantasies.

Julia is then able to see her fantasies in a more generous light. If they function well and help her get aroused, she can count them as positives. Just because she doesn't find them socially acceptable doesn't mean that it's wrong to have them. Fantasies don't give us any information about a person's needs and character. But as we've seen, there is always a connection between body and mind.

I ask Julia how she masturbates. It turns out that she needs a lot of tension. She breathes shallowly, doesn't move, and places her vibrator to the right of her clitoris. She says that she needs a very strong vibrator. I explain that masturbating this way is very likely to give rise to fantasies like hers. Extreme tension often leads to feelings like fear and anger.

By wanting to change or get rid of her fantasies, Julia is putting unnecessary pressure on herself. But as she develops and refines her physical perception, the images in her mind will start to change too. She has to start with her arousal pattern if she wants her fantasies to change.

Julia is reassured to hear that her fantasies don't mean anything about her personality. Above all, she'd like not to absolutely need them to come to orgasm with her partner. In the following months, she comes to see me regularly and we work step-by-step on the way she arouses herself. She gets to know her body better and is soon able to increase her arousal in a variety of ways. She learns to enjoy herself and begins to move more—both when masturbating and during sex. After a while, Julia notices that her perception and her fantasies are changing. I suggest that she not keep too close watch on her fantasies, because that will lead to tension as well. It's better if she devotes herself fully to concentrating on the exercises. And when new fantasies arise, I advise her to simply accept them, and then after a while to observe them with fresh eyes.

(Step 7)

SWING IT!

The Pelvic
Swing

YOU'RE NOW STARTING to move more when you masturbate, and maybe during sex as well. You're circling
your hips, tilting your pelvis back and forth. Maybe
you've already noticed that the kind of movement you use
has an influence on your arousal:

* Fluid movement of the whole body distributes arousal
  widely and increases desire and physical enjoyment.

* Pelvic circles during penetration are a good way to massage the vaginal walls.

✳ Rocking the pelvis (the so-called pelvic swing, which we'll learn in this chapter) channels and strengthens the arousal.

✳ From must-come to can-come: the real goal isn't the orgasm itself, but rather the pleasurable and satisfying path toward it. The more you concentrate on your enjoyment and varied ways of increasing your arousal, the more the orgasm will happen "on its own."

IN THE LAST chapters we learned how to sense and increase arousal. In order to get to orgasm, we need to add a little something extra. The intensity of the arousal has to increase so much that the orgasm reflex is triggered. For example, the muscle tension has to increase, the touch has to become stronger or quicker, the breath or the fantasies have to grow more intense. And that's where the pelvic swing comes into play. In this tilting movement, the pelvis is thrust back and forth along an axis. The body above the pelvis doesn't move. This first distributes the arousal and then channels it. The reason this is helpful is that if the intensity isn't additionally increased near the end of sex, you may have a lot of sensation for a long period of time and be very close to orgasm, but never reach the climax. The pelvic swing can be used in any position, and doesn't have to be a big movement. You can move your pelvis quickly or slowly.

With the pelvic swing, you'll first practice alone, as usual. At first it will be easier if you take your time and make the movements either very small, or very big, but slow. Move your head now and then to keep your neck from getting tense. At first, the swing might feel like a gymnastics exercise. Over time, you'll start to do this motion so naturally that you'll be able to concentrate completely on your sensations. Start in the position that you usually use to masturbate. For many women, this will be a pelvic swing lying on the back.

The pelvic swing lying down

LIE ON YOUR back and bend your knees, with your feet flat on the bed or other surface. Place a hand under your lower back, with your palm face up—this will help you to feel the movement better. Push your back against the bed so that your hand is pushed flat. After you've practiced for a while and know the exercise fairly well, you can simply lay your hand next to your body. Breathe out while you're doing this.

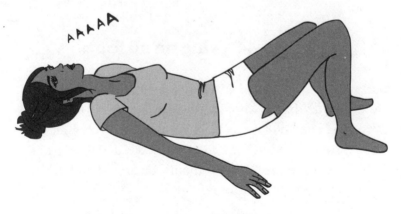

Now, shift your weight so that the hollow of your back lifts away from your hand, breathing in as you do so. When you've internalized the motion, you can take your hand away. It's ideal for the muscles of your stomach and buttocks to remain relaxed during the exercise—you can test this by laying a land on your stomach or butt.

Even when lying down, try to steer the movement from your pelvis: tilt it forward and then backward. Swing slowly back and forth, breathing evenly in and out.

The pelvic swing on all fours

ON A COMFORTABLE surface, rest on your hands and knees, with hands shoulder-width apart. Alternatively, you can bend your arms and support yourself on your forearms. Now arch your back so that it's rounded upward. It's good to exaggerate the movement a bit at first. While your back is arched, breathe out.

Then let your spine sink downward so that it forms a U-shape, breathing in.

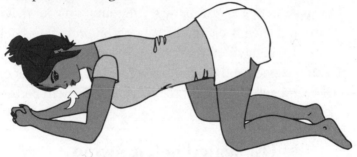

Return to the arched back, then again to the U-shape. Repeat the movement several times and try to do it smoothly rather than jerkily.

In the second step, try to steer the movement from your pelvis. Tip your pelvis so that your sex parts come forward and move toward your stomach: this forms the arched back. Then tip the pelvis back, and you'll find yourself in a U-shape. Doing this motion fluidly, imagine taking something into your vagina, sucking it upward and into you. When you arch your back, you're taking in the object (it could be a penis, dildo, or finger). When you release your back down, you're letting it go. Important: don't concentrate too hard on the right position and the perfect motion. Just try out the swing and observe how you feel while doing it. Don't try to do everything all at once— breathing, position, and motion. Just go step-by-step and notice precisely what you feel. Sensing your body is much more important than perfect execution!

Now let's try the whole thing standing: Stand in front of a mirror with your feet about shoulder-width apart. Bend your knees slightly, and don't let them lock. This will give your upper body the flexibility you need. Now make the same movement you just made on all fours: tip your pelvis forward and then back again. When you arch your back, breathe out, and when you stick your butt out, breathe in. You can put one hand on your lower belly and another on your lower back if you want to feel the movement better.

The seated pelvic swing

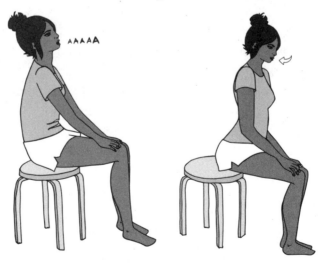

SIT COMFORTABLY IN a chair and tip your pelvis back and forth. Make the same movement as in the other positions, only it will be smaller, since you're not able to move as freely.

You can practice the seated pelvic swing anywhere—in the subway, at school, or at the office. You just swing almost imperceptibly back and forth and move slightly into the arch or the U-shape. Here, too, imagine your vagina taking something in when it's tilted forward and drawing it back out when you tilt it back. You can also use this exercise when, for example, you can't think anymore at work, or when you're nervous before flying—whenever you want to put your body in a different state.

The pelvic swing in cowgirl position

FORM A PILLOW or blanket into a mound about as big as a person's torso. Sit comfortably on top of it with bent legs.

Since the cowgirl position can be hard on the knees, you first have to figure out the best angle for you. You can prop your hands to the left and right of the pillow. You can also sit upright and put your hands on your thighs. Now make the swinging motion. You thrust—or better, swing—your pelvis back and forth, just like in the other exercises, breathing in and out as you do so.

THE PELVIC SWING is one of the movements that can help you to increase and intensify arousal. You don't need to swing the whole time you're having sex or masturbating. When you make circling and flowing motions occasionally with your pelvis and whole body, you can distribute the arousal better and enjoy the sex even more. So let your hips circle now and then, or draw figure eights with your pelvis. Or imagine that you're a vine, and stretch and twist your whole body in every direction. This will also ensure that your upper body and head don't tense up. Over time, the movement will become automatic, and you won't be able to imagine sex without it.

Exercises

1. Practice the pelvic swing. On its own—not while masturbating or having sex. It's not about arousal at this point but rather about getting your body to understand and internalize the movement, so that you don't have to concentrate on it anymore. If you lie on your back to masturbate, work the pelvic swing into your routine in this position first. Try to steer the motion from your

back, and not with your legs or the muscles of your buttocks. And during the exercise, imagine picking something up and drawing it in with the vagina, and then letting it go. When the movement functions well in this position, go on to the next position and practice it that way at least four times. Practice the seated pelvic swing whenever you're sitting and waiting somewhere. Repeat the pelvic swing in various positions so often that you no longer have to think about it and your body makes the motion automatically. But be careful—don't try to do everything at once. Every time you practice, just concentrate on one of the four positions.

2. Place your finger in the entrance of the vagina (while you're doing the pelvic swing exercise, if you want) and see if you feel the desire to take it farther inside. You can move your finger, or just keep it still inside you. If you want to practice while you're aroused and you find the arousal subsiding, take your finger out and see what happens. Then arouse yourself as you usually do. If you're lying on your back and feel like your arm isn't long enough, put a pillow under your pelvis, or lie on your stomach and curl your legs up underneath you like a ball.

Good to know

What's the advantage of the pelvic swing and other kinds of movement over different ways of increasing arousal?

If you increase the tension in your body in order to heighten your arousal, and try to keep this up over a long period of time, you'll eventually start to experience numbness because your muscles have been tensed for so long. A lot of tension can work well for a quickie, but it doesn't work so well for long-drawn-out sex. For example, anyone who primarily arouses themselves visually relies on intensification of the visual stimulants. Over time, the images have to become more extreme, because the brain gets used to what it's already seen and craves more intense stimulation. Fantasies, too, have to become more intense over time—more brutal, or more specific—because they start to get "worn out." These intensifications, which trigger the orgasm reflex, eventually exhaust themselves. Continual movement of the whole body, and especially of the pelvis, is less strenuous for the muscles, and therefore more suitable for long sex. And it's a technique that can still be used as we grow older, as well. In addition, it makes the sensations more intense, because the body—including the sex parts—receives more blood flow.

Do I have to involve my partner? Or do I just keep having sex with him as we usually do?

Here there's no right or wrong answer. You can use your new discoveries with your partner, or you can keep practicing and trying things out alone and not integrate what you learn into sex just yet. It's completely up to you. I usually advise my patients to just try things out and see how they and their partner react.

When I do the second exercise and put my finger in the entrance to my vagina, my arousal subsides. What can I do?

If you were used to arousing yourself without touching your vagina, it might be that your finger distracts you so much that your arousal disappears or never even arises. If that's the case, stimulate yourself as you usually do, without the finger in your vagina. When your arousal increases, put your finger in. Alternate until your finger no longer bothers you. This exercise is easier when you're alone. You're in control of your finger, but your partner's is less predictable.

At the same time, you can become more familiar with your vagina and the entrance to it. Try to notice it as you go about your daily routine; take more time on your vagina when you shower and moisturize yourself. The more your vagina is used to being touched, the less jarring it will feel to be touched when you're aroused.

My arms are too short! I can't get my finger in.

If you find lying on your back uncomfortable, try on all fours—this is the best way to reach your sex parts with your hand. Or put a pillow under your butt or upper body—this makes it easier to reach your vagina with your hands. It can also help to lie on your side.

Why should I use my finger and not a dildo, which is more the size of a penis?

You learn more quickly with a finger, because your finger is connected to your brain, just like your vagina. Thus, the brain is doubly stimulated. A dildo has no connection to the brain. Using one does have advantages, however: a dildo can help you reach spots that your fingers can't, because they're too short—the cervix, for example. I suggest practicing with your finger at first, and alternating now and then with a dildo—which looks like a vibrator, but can't vibrate.

CASE STUDY
Jeanette

JEANETTE IS IN HER early fifties and comes to me regularly over the course of several months. At first she found it hard to bring herself to practice regularly, but over time she understood the exercises better and grew more motivated. It only took a little while for her to feel more when she increased her movement during masturbation, and she could get very aroused. But as soon as she moved more with her partner, her arousal fell apart and orgasm seemed distant.

She's annoyed and unsure if she'll ever achieve an orgasm with her partner—or alone. She's been at it for a while and keeps on trying, but says with frustration, "It's seems like it's time now! It has to start working."

I tell Jeanette that including movement in sex with a partner is the biggest challenge of the whole process. And that the switch from being passive to becoming active can be difficult for the brain as well. I suggest she take a step to the side instead of a step forward. She should have sex with her partner a few times the way they used to do it, so that she can enjoy being with him more again. I show Jeanette how far she's already come—and that gives her courage. She sets aside the topic of movement for a while, and I advise her to start with it again only when she feels the desire to. And when she does, she should take tiny steps and move only slightly at first.

I furthermore suggest that she concentrate less on the movement and more on her sensations. If you're not in the here and now, you'll lose sight of the goal. It's common for women to get impatient near the finish line and expect the orgasm to just finally "work." And so, after weeks where they haven't thought very concretely about their orgasm, they start to focus much more on it again. This often ties them up in knots and makes them tense and frustrated.

A few weeks later, I ask Jeanette if she's started moving more again during masturbation and sex, and how it's going. She says yes and says she didn't even notice it at first, but she had started moving again unconsciously. When she thinks about it, she realizes that she actually can't *not* move anymore.

She still hasn't had an orgasm through sex, but she doesn't mind. She no longer feels under time pressure. She can sense that she's on the right track because she can feel how much sex and her desire have already changed. "I don't *have* to have an orgasm anymore," Jeanette says. "I already enjoy the whole thing much more."

(Step 8)

BE MORE SELF-CENTERED!

Pay Attention to You

I'S IMPORTANT TO learn to be more self-centered in bed and to pay attention to your needs. As a patient of mine recently put it so perfectly: "The more selfish I am and the more I concentrate on myself, the better sex I have and . . . the better the sex is for my partner, as well." That might sound strange at first. Self-interest will help your partner? In books and magazines, we read about how to be the perfect lover, what techniques we have to master, how we can best please our partner, and now we're supposed to forget about it all and just think about ourselves? Yes! Absolutely! Because the more you take what you want, the more you'll enjoy the sex and the more you'll want it. And that's extremely attractive! A woman who surrenders to her desire and takes what she wants—every partner wants that! It's a classic win-win situation.

The more you concentrate on your pleasure, the less important it becomes for your partner to move just so. And that frees him or her from the pressure to do everything perfectly. Your partner can also concentrate on his or her own sensations. When you're more self-focused, you're no longer completely dependent on your partner for your arousal—and that's the goal. Then it becomes less important how he moves or what she does, and in every situation, you can take what you need to have amazing sex.

At this point with my clients I often talk about sexual responsiveness as a tree. Your knowledge of your body and your practice provide the roots that make the tree strong. Without strong roots, the tree can easily be damaged by a storm or strong wind. But if these roots are well developed, wind, drought, or other stresses won't affect the tree as much. The more you feel, the better you know your body, the more you've developed it and can influence it, the less you're affected by external factors like stress with your partner or at work.

But how can you manage this? First of all: allow yourself to be selfish. This sounds easier than it is. But it's doable. Think about yourself during sex! Try not to ask yourself if your partner likes what you're doing together. Instead, ask yourself if *you* like what you're doing together. If you're primarily concerned with doing what's right and good for the other person, your ability to perceive your own sensations will be reduced. Therefore: concentrate on your body, or even on just one specific part of your body. What does your vagina feel, where is your hand, what does your clitoris feel?

Second: move more! The more you move, the more connected you are to yourself and your arousal. Try in general to move more, like you practiced when masturbating. Notice how it feels. Does the movement help you to feel more? What do you sense? What do you feel when you make circular, quick, or slow movements?

Your partner will notice that you're concentrating more on yourself. It's important to know that couples are usually at roughly the same stage in their sexual development. A woman often thinks that her partner is incredibly versatile and advanced, and that she only has to work on herself, because her partner can more easily react to new patterns and movements. But a man's limits also often only become visible when the woman makes changes. In other words: if for years a woman has been very tense during sex and simply absorbed the man's thrusts, the extent of his versatility will become clear when she starts to move. Is he able to respond to this new kind of sex? Or can he only come through monotonous pounding? If a man actually isn't so "advanced," he'll quickly reach his limits and perhaps will also want to expand his repertoire. He can go through the same process as the woman and learn to know and sensitize his sex parts better. You'll find more on this in the chapter for men toward the end of the book.

Ultimately, as it is with women, so it is with men too: anyone who's come to orgasm for years with great tension and through very specific stimulation will at first start to lose their arousal when this pattern is disturbed. The man, just like the woman, has likely developed one or several patterns and methods of arousal. If the woman changes her pattern, he'll probably have to adapt his, too. Perhaps he's always needed a particular kind of friction in the vagina to come. When his partner suddenly moves, the vagina will shift or expand and the friction will diminish. It's therefore perfectly possible that he'll lose his erection occasionally and will have to expand his repertoire as well.

How can you support your partner through this process? You can show and explain to him what's changed for you and what you like. Your partner isn't clairvoyant—he won't simply pick up on what's different for you, what you like, and what you now need. When talking about sex, there are a few rules to keep in mind—otherwise it can quickly become a teacher-student situation. This could set up a power dynamic that hampers true communication and progress and alienates your partner. Here are a few tips:

* Be honest with your partner. If you're unsettled or anxious, it's good to talk to him about it. It won't help to tell him you liked something if in fact you didn't.

* Don't tell your partner what you didn't like right after sex, when he's lying in bed, exhausted and satisfied. If you're unsatisfied or frustrated, talk about it another time. Maybe even set up a specific time to talk about it.

* Pay attention to the way you phrase things. If you reproach your partner, he or she may feel attacked, and may attack back, or else withdraw. Try something like: "I liked this and that. I'd also like it if . . ." or "Next time, should we try doing this more?" rather than "You did that wrong!" "You really could try harder to . . ." or "You never . . ." The "compliment sandwich" is also helpful: first something positive, then criticism, and then again something positive to conclude.

* And finally: talking about sex is also a matter of practice. At first, it's hard for many people, both women and men. But the more often you do it, the more you get used to it, and soon it will become normal, or perhaps even erotic and arousing for you.

BE PATIENT WITH yourself, with your partner, with the two of you as a team, and above all with the sex you have together! Don't expect big changes at first. The sex will change bit by bit, but it requires time. You may so far have noticed quick changes and progress. Up till now, you've practiced alone, so you could control all the movements yourself. Sex together, on the other hand, harbors a great potential for distraction. Keep this in mind—sex together is a matter of practice too. The same rules apply: Don't expect everything at once. Change things step-by-step. A sense of humor can be a great help, and it can also ensure that even with mishaps, slipups, and downright busts, you'll still have fun.

Exercises

1. Place one or more fingers on your vulva. If you like, get them wet first with saliva, lube, or oil. Instead of moving your fingers, move your pelvis. Swing and make circles. Think of a cat that wants to be petted—you just have to hold your hand out and it will rub up against it where it wants to be touched. Do it like a cat, holding your hand still and getting the stimulation you want by moving your body. Notice what you feel, and whether it feels different than when you lie still. You can also place one or more fingers in your vagina. Just keep your hand still and use the pelvic swing to make your fingers slide in and out. Practice this several times a week.

2. Practice your self-focus! When you're having sex, try to be conscious of what feels good and what doesn't. When your attention wanders to your partner, direct it back toward yourself. And even more important: move more during sex, so that you get what feels good to you.

Good to know

Won't I be emotionally absent if I just concentrate on myself during sex? Won't the sex be impersonal if I'm getting lost in my own world?

You're not absent—you're just focusing on yourself, and on your sensations and experience with your partner. If you're thinking about your grocery list or feeling annoyed by your partner during sex, you're much more absent. But sure, at first your partner may be confused to see you moving more or taking more care of yourself. In the long run, he'll benefit from this too.

Apart from that, many men say it's important to them to feel how aroused their partner is. If two people lie in bed, each waiting for the other to become aroused, not much will happen. The arousal of one person has a positive effect on the arousal of the other.

Won't the sex be worse if I'm more selfish?

The sex will change, but it certainly won't get worse. Over time, it will get much, much better—because you'll enjoy it more, and that will turn your partner on. By concentrating more on your sensations, you're more in the here and now, and you can react more to your partner's arousal. Neither of you will be distracted by unerotic things like your last credit card bill. But yes: improving sex means changing it. And with change comes risk. If you do what you've always done, you at least know what you're getting. It takes courage to trade something familiar for something new. Dare to try it.

What should I do if my partner complains? What if he liked it better the way it was before, because he prefers hard thrusting?

It's important to understand why your partner is complaining. Usually it's not because the new ways themselves don't suit him, but rather because he's afraid of losing his erection. Try to be understanding, and encourage him to push his limits as well. You can learn how in the chapter for men at the end of this book. It's not a matter of banning hard thrusts from the repertoire entirely—they're a nice possibility, but it would be a shame if they were the only option.

Bettina

BETTINA IS THIRTY-NINE AND has been with her partner for a long time. They have a good relationship and have regular sex, though mostly when he wants it. He wants to have sex more often than she does—it's simply more fun for him. It's not a major problem in the relationship, but Bettina worries that it will become one if things continue this way. She's afraid he'll eventually complain that he always has to take the first step. And so she comes to see me.

Bettina knows what to expect when they have sex. It's pleasant and nice for her, but she could also do without it. Above all, she has sex "for his sake." Therefore, she concentrates primarily on her partner. Since sex is so important to him, she wants him to enjoy it as much as possible. And ultimately, she wants to be a good lover.

I ask Bettina to stroke my arm. First, in a way that she thinks will be pleasant for me. Then I ask her to do it again and to concentrate only on what her fingers sense and not on whether it feels good to me or not. After this exercise, Bettina can see that when her attention is on the other person, it's only logical that she feels less and gets less out of the experience.

Bettina has to learn to think of herself more. But she worries that if she does so, she'll stop being a good lover: that her partner will lose interest in her and not like sex with her anymore. She's worried that he'll find her strange and selfish. Over the course of many conversations, and with the help of Bettina's increasing experience, we manage to make these worries smaller and smaller.

After a while, she tells me that she's started to perceive everyday touches more—when she and her partner see each other, she nuzzles up close to him, and it feels good.

After a few weeks, she recounts the last time they had sex: She primarily focused on herself. At first, she felt very egotistical. But suddenly she realized that she was very aroused and could enjoy the sex more than ever. She was almost shocked. After the sex, she worried that her partner would notice that she was lost in her own world and her own arousal. "But," she tells me with a smile, "the next morning my boyfriend told me that last night he found me hotter than he had in a long time. Because I let myself go in a way he'd never experienced."

(Step 9)

SWING IT TOGETHER!

Movement in Duet

MANY WOMEN REPORT that they feel a lot when they move more, and they almost reach climax but can't quite get over the edge. As mentioned in the previous chapters, in order for the orgasm reflex to be released, the arousal has to be intensified one final time. Perhaps you've already noticed that you do this automatically when you masturbate: right before the climax, you increase the pressure through your legs, or you move your fingers faster. Maybe you put your vibrator directly on your clitoris or your fantasies get more intense.

It works the same way when you want to learn to come through penetration. The arousal has to be turned up another notch. Movement is important to make this happen during sex with a partner. If, for example, you've mastered the pelvic swing and feel good about the motion, you can work it into sex with your partner. It can be used in almost any position, even when you're fairly "trapped" and can barely move. Try to move your pelvis so your vagina can take in the penis, just like you practiced with your finger. In theory, the penis can just remain still, and you pull it in with the movement of your pelvis. It glides by turns in and then out again. Ask your partner not to move and see how it works. When you control the movements with your pelvis, you can also control the speed.

The main reason many people find sex with their partner more fulfilling than the arousal they feel from masturbation is the emotional pleasure they get with a partner, which we already investigated in Step 2 with the arousal diagrams. As a quick reminder: an orgasm is a release of sexual arousal paired with a release on the emotional level—in other words, a release of feelings and desire. When the orgasm reflex is triggered, the muscles of the pelvic floor contract once or several times rhythmically. After this purely physical orgasmic release, the tension in the body and the blood flow to the sex parts quickly decrease. Physical arousal proceeds like so:

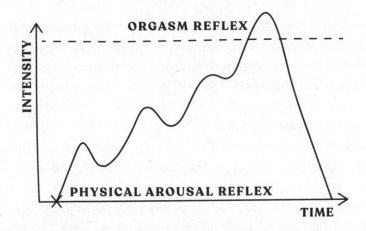

Ideally, during sex, in addition to the physical arousal, emotional tension and pleasure also grow, to the point where they're finally released in an orgasm. The more you're able to emotionally let go in the upper half of your body, the more intense your orgasm will feel. But what does this release of feelings look like? Some women express their emotions through their voice—they scream when they reach orgasm, laugh, or even cry. This emotional release is therefore reflected in the chest, shoulders, throat, neck, head, and/or voice.

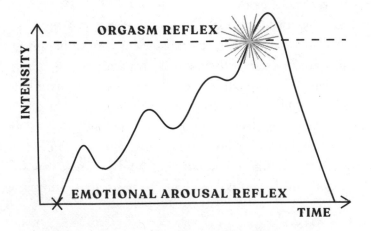

WHEN WOMEN ARE asked how they experience an orgasm, the descriptions vary widely. This shows that the line between purely physical release and an all-encompassing orgasm is a fluid one. On one end of the spectrum, a woman could feel a slight pulsing in her sex parts, or a pleasant sense of release. At the other end, women report fireworks of warmth and light, cosmic flight and ecstatic raptures. In such cases, the whole body, mind, and spirit take part in the orgasm.

Such experiences sound extremely appealing! To get there, you have to be able to let go on an emotional level in the upper half of your body—and that has to be learned, especially since the neck and jaw tend to hold a lot of tension. It can help to open your mouth slightly during sex. This helps the jaw to relax, and that in turn relaxes the head. When the mouth is open, the pelvic floor muscles are also more relaxed, since the jaw and pelvic floor muscles are indirectly connected. Breathing is important, too. I recommend breathing deep into your belly during sex: when you breathe out, the pelvis goes out, and when you breathe in, it goes back. Make sure that your mouth is open when you breathe out.

Last but not least: use your voice. Moan, just to try it out. If your voice is clear, the muscles of your upper body and jaw are relaxed. If they sound strained, you're tense, which isn't ideal. Moaning loudly makes many women uncomfortable: it's like they have a little police officer in their heads that forbids them to be too loud. Don't listen to him—he's a killjoy! It might not come naturally for you to moan loudly, but vocalizing can be a great way to really get into it and come closer to your goal. Through the movement and sounds that you make, you can hardly *not* let go. By breathing into your belly and moaning, you experience and enjoy the sex with your whole body, because the interaction of muscles and the alternation of tension and release helps distribute the arousal throughout your whole body. You can make your movements while shutting out the external world, only connected to your sensations. Think of the saying: "Dance like nobody's watching."

Throughout the previous steps, it was okay for everything you learned and did to feel unerotic. By incorporating moaning and letting go, you're adding much more pleasure and eroticism, both to your masturbation and to sex as a couple. You're now starting to integrate what you've learned into your sexuality with your partner, where the erotic plays a very different role—and a very important one! If you notice that you're losing your arousal because you're thinking too much about the exercises and trying to do everything right, go back to your old, familiar ways. Just do what you (and the two of you) feel like doing. Some other time, try adding what you've learned into your sex together, bit by bit, and be patient if it doesn't work right away, despite the fact that you've already gotten good at doing it alone.

It's important to remember that from now on, you should be able to choose to do what you feel like. If you want to come in two minutes and then relax, masturbation with a vibrator is definitely a good choice. Sometimes fast food is just the right thing. But if you want, you can also enjoy a ten-course meal. That's what you're practicing for!

Exercises

1. Integrate movement into sex. If it gets too complicated and you're too in your head, concentrate more on your sensations and try not to think too much about perfect execution of the pelvic swing. The most important thing is that you feel more.

2. Start moving your upper body when you masturbate, and start using your voice and making your breath audible. Notice how this changes your experience.

Good to know

Is it possible to have quick sex together and come to orgasm?

Quickies can be wonderfully arousing! But if the man just pounds away, the woman will probably be excited, but not feel much in the vagina, other than perhaps movement around the entrance. More varied motion of the penis in the vagina can stimulate the walls of the vagina well even during quick sex, which can be very arousing on a physical level.

I'm using the pelvic swing in sex but still not coming to orgasm. What am I doing wrong?

When you're practicing, it's never about doing something wrong but rather about understanding what you do, when and how, with your body, and how this affects your experience. So: What's the level of your arousal? How far are you able to raise it? What happens then? Many of my patients are fairly impatient, and at a certain point they want to give up. If you start in an unaroused state, it can take up to fifteen minutes until your sex parts are warmed up. And if you move a lot because you want to come, it can take even more time for the arousal to increase to the crucial point. It depends on how aroused you are and how well your vagina is trained.

There's an additional challenge in sex with a partner: not everyone has a great sense of time. And many women quickly start to feel guilty. They think things like: "My boyfriend has been at it between my legs for ten minutes already and I still haven't come. Poor guy, his tongue must be about to fall off!" They concentrate too little on themselves and think almost exclusively about their partners. Therefore: even if you're using this book mainly to learn how to have an orgasm through intercourse—pursuing this as a goal—it's important to see the way you get there as a goal in itself, one that's just as important. The more you feel, the more the journey becomes the destination. The real goal is for you to be able to enjoy every minute so much that your climax is only *one* important component of the sex you have. The orgasm will become less important because the journey there is so intense. The more you feel in every individual moment, the more you forget that you have a goal at all.

Claudia and Markus

CLAUDIA COMES TO SEE me with her boyfriend, Markus. She was in the orgasm group I started with my colleague and she got a lot out of the exercises. Now when having sex with her partner she feels much more connected to herself, she moves more, and her enjoyment has increased.

But trying out her new abilities with her boyfriend has become a source of conflict, because Markus is used to just "pounding away." With Claudia's development, this no longer works, because she wants to move. She wants him to thrust more slowly, so she can feel more. To Markus, the sex is boring and no longer feels "natural." They come to see me because they both want to find a solution.

As we talk, it becomes clear that Markus's main problem isn't actually that he finds the "new" sex unnatural and boring, but that he's worried that he won't be able to keep his erection. This fear is justified: with the pelvic swing, he feels less friction than when they "screw hard." It's completely understandable that he can't constantly keep up his erection with a different kind of sex. During short, quick penetration, the man is usually more tensed and feels a lot of friction, which increases his arousal, but reduces his pleasure and enjoyment. In addition, the way Markus used to have sex with Claudia, he doesn't have to be able to keep his erection too long, because the sex doesn't usually last as long as it does when she incorporates the pelvic swing. It's a eureka moment for Markus to learn that many men can't keep up an erection the whole time—nor must they.

I try to explain to Markus that the situation can be an opportunity for him as well. He too can perceive and feel more with the pelvic swing and with relaxed, passionate sex. That sounds interesting to him, and he wants to try it out and open himself up to it. He practices the swing motion for himself and concentrates more on his sensations. Thanks to the exercises, over time he finds the new sex much more intense, even when his penis isn't hard the whole time. He's no longer insecure when the arousal comes in waves during longer sex instead of just increasing in a straight line.

A few weeks later, they come back to me and I notice right away that something has changed: they seem much more in love. They laugh more, seem more carefree, and are much more affectionate with each other. This is a typical effect. When two people start to have a different kind of sex and are less "hard" and more playful, loving, and gentle toward each other in bed, this playfulness and affection comes out in the rest of the relationship as well.

Today, Markus and Claudia have a fulfilling sex life. They don't always have long, sensual sex. Sometimes they have sex like they used to. They "screw" the way they did for years. There's nothing wrong with that. This kind of sex has its own appeal, and it's part of their repertoire; it gives their sex life variety. But they both find the ability to change it up very enriching.

(Step 10)

BLASTING OFF TOGETHER

A Lifetime of Good Sex

THERE ARE COUPLES who have good, sensual sex with each other for years or even decades. What do they do differently? Do they fight less? Are they healthier? Less stressed? Do they have fewer problems in their daily lives? Is their relationship more harmonious? Do they have unproblematic kids, or no kids at all? Do they not have annoying in-laws?

The major difference is this: both partners want to have sex because they know it does them good. Because they find it hot, because it makes them feel close to each other, because it's a good way to relax... Each partner has their reasons, and gets the maximum out of sex. Each has their own strong need for sex and physicality and wants to satisfy it. The reason for this is that the connections between their sex parts and brains are well developed, and so every touch leads to a great deal of arousal, pleasure, and joy. Therefore both partners are satisfied, confident, and relaxed during and after sex. It's the kind of feeling people also get from a good run or a great meal.

The fact remains: not many couples have such a fulfilled, active sex life over the course of many years. Yet most couples start out with similar basic conditions. When two people get to know each other, they usually try out a lot of things. Over time, they leave behind the things that don't work perfectly or aren't fun right away. Many couples' repertoire shrinks to three or four positions, a few techniques, a particular speed. If anything is changed, the whole system falls apart. If you change, your partner has to change too. That takes courage! At first, your partner might feel uncomfortable. Or the situation can be embarrassing because everything doesn't immediately work the way you want it to. Improving sex and expanding your repertoire means that both partners have to be brave and willing to change. Both partners have to learn to articulate their desires and to learn to make suggestions.

This is easier said than done. For many people, sex is a very intimate and delicate thing, and the last realm in which they want to offend or be criticized. In addition, female sexuality in particular is still strongly bound by shame and is often taboo. Some women think they're not allowed to ask for sex. In some relationships this goes so far that the woman thinks she'd lose face if she revealed herself to be a woman with desires. There's still a persistent myth that women's sex drives aren't as strong as those of men. That's completely absurd and incorrect, but it makes it difficult for some women to admit their sexual wants and needs. They don't want to seem like instinct-driven beings—just modestly sensual ones. Social norms that show us which pigeonhole we belong in and make us doubt ourselves are to blame. In many cases, these worries and fears make it more difficult to implement what you've learned with your partner. For some women, this has a physical effect as well: they freeze up during sex and feel less.

The party principle

WHENEVER A PATIENT tells me that the doubting voices in her head are getting too loud, telling her she mustn't, shouldn't, couldn't possibly, and making her tense and passive during sex, I recommend the party principle.

Imagine you're invited to a party, but you don't feel like going. What do you do? Usually you're nice and go anyway. You were invited, after all. Now you're at the party, and even if you don't find it particularly great, and the people there aren't your best friends, how the evening goes is largely up to you. Either you can hide in a corner and be bored to tears, or you can step onto the dance floor and dance wildly. If you do the latter, you have a much better chance of having a good night. Because you've suddenly cast off all your inhibitions? Because you suddenly don't care if people give you funny looks? No!

But when you move intensively, your brain loses the capacity to worry. With automatic movements, your brain can be concentrated on your thoughts and worries, but complicated movements claim your mental focus. If you're shy, just start moving carefully. Even then you'll feel a difference.

The same goes for sex: when your whole body is involved, you're forced to concentrate on yourself and your sensations. Your brain has no more space to worry. The voices in your head fall silent.

The conditions don't always have to be perfect

PERFECTIONISM CAN BE another challenge. Some women think they can only have sex when the apartment is clean, their legs are shaved, and they're feeling perfectly in sync with their partner. Such conditions are rarely met at the same time. Maybe the apartment is clean and your legs are shaved, but then your partner comes home and isn't as affectionate as you expected—and so you give up on sex. Just because one factor is missing. But with the ten-step plan, these conditions will naturally grow less important. The greater your physical need for sex, the less important all the external conditions will be.

Many women tell me that they understand this perfectly well yet are still struggling with the implementation. They know in their head that all the conditions are rarely met, and that they don't actually have to be, but emotionally they have a hard time adjusting, much as they might want to. The explanation for this is fairly logical and once again lies in our sympathetic nervous system. The countless tasks and duties that we want to complete every day to the best of our abilities put our bodies in fight-or-flight mode. Then, if something with our partner doesn't go just according to plan, our natural defense mechanisms kick in. Sex and tenderness are distant and feel impossible. But it doesn't have to be that way. In the previous steps you've gained the tools to disrupt fight-or-flight mode. The trick in such moments is to recognize that you've slipped into an automatic biological pattern that you can actively break—if you want to. The best way to do that is with movement and breathing.

At this point, some of my patients argue that despite the ten steps and the fact that they've gotten to know their bodies better, they and their partners aren't constantly all over each other. The crux of the matter is this: many couples have sex according to a principle of spontaneity. Our society is ruled by the myth that only spontaneous sex is good sex. But in fact, many realms of life no longer have room for spontaneity, nor do we always want it. We plan our free time, decide in advance when we're going to exercise and meet friends; we set aside time to spend with our family. Why should sex be an exception? Why don't we look forward to planned sex the way we look forward to a meal with our best friend? Or yoga class? Anticipation has an important energy. Why shouldn't we use it for sex?

My tip for everyone who's struggling because of the spontaneity principle (which means most couples) is to put a few sex-evenings per week in your calendar. Important note: it doesn't have to be fantastic every time. If you have sex regularly, it doesn't matter so much if it's a little boring now and then. Like when you just eat a simple sandwich between three amazing dinners.

What can you do to make your sex more active and your relationship more erotic?

* **Be brave:** Learn to have confidence in each other. It's okay if your partner doesn't immediately like a new technique or is put off by a new idea. There has to be space for that too.

* **Be active:** The longer two people are together, the less they move during sex. Statistically, couples are much more active during sex at the beginning of a relationship. So move! You don't have to do crazy gymnastics moves: even small, slow movements can help you toward your goal.

* **Rediscover each other:** Over time, many people's patterns generally grow narrower and more specific. They try fewer things, or they just run through the same tried-and-true program. In other words: they get lazy. It's important here to get active again and to rediscover your partner's body—even if you think you already know each other inside and out.

* **Don't always shoot for the moon:** Give each other massages without having sex afterward. Have a long make-out session but don't go any further. Integrate more touching into your daily lives, and thus increase your desire for more.

* **Don't expect a miracle:** Passion doesn't come back all on its own. But even little changes can make a big difference: Getting up and going to greet your partner when she comes home instead of just calling out "hello" from the kitchen. Giving your partner a warm, tight hug. Giving him a real kiss instead of just a peck.

* **Don't make harmony a condition for desire:** Some women say they can only have sex with their partners when everything's just right. Try to separate this connection between perfect harmony and desire. Sexual desire can also happen when every detail hasn't been worked out first. See what happens if you hug each other when you both actually feel like the other person is being an idiot.

* And finally, the most important advice: **Be patient with each other!**

Exercises

1. This exercise was invented by the systemic sex therapist Ulrich Clement, and I like to use it with my patients. The short version can work like this: You and your partner each write down your sexual wishes, or even a whole ideal sexual scenario, on a piece of paper, then put what you've written in separate envelopes. In the next step, talk about whether you want to open the other person's envelope, and what doing so would mean. You don't have to open them, and if you do, you don't have to put them into practice—that's not the

main point. Rather, this should help you figure out what you want together, and how you feel about your partner's sexual desires. Do you really want to know about them? Are you really interested in them in the long term?

If you want to go further with this exercise, I highly recommend Ulrich Clement's books, though they are currently only available in German.

2. Use the party principle. When you hear critical voices in your head telling you you're not allowed to be a sex-craving being, take active notice of them and decide whether you want to give them space. If you don't want to give them space, give *yourself* space: Move as much as possible, even if you don't really feel like it. Take initiative! Be twice as active! Be particularly passionate! Imagine you're in the middle of the dance floor having the time of your life, even if you originally wanted to stay home on the couch.

Good to know

What should I do if I don't feel like sex—for example, if we just had a big fight?

Of course you don't *have* to have sex then, or ever. But maybe you've noticed that you can use your body to influence your feelings, and not just the other way around. Anger, bad moods, or stress can change for the better if you and your partner have a nice, passionate time on a physical level. You don't need to be in perfect harmony for that.

Having sex despite a fight can have a totally positive effect on your relationship: on the one hand, because sex and orgasms help you to relax, and on the other hand, because it's a way to come closer to each other again. But how can you open yourself to sex when you feel no desire? By throwing yourself into it even if you don't feel like it. Think of the party principle: go to your partner, make out with him, stroke him tenderly. That way, you stop the down-ward spiral. Of course I'm not saying you should have sex against your will. It's just about giving yourself or each other a chance to see whether your appetite grows when you taste the food. Like the words one of my students has as a tattoo: "When you cuddle, you repair each other."

What should I do when my partner doesn't feel like it?

After a while, many couples end up in a pattern of "reverse seduction." This subject would be enough to fill a book, but in short what it means is this: the partners blame each other, are easily offended, and have very specific ideas about how they want to be seduced. But seduction actually means: "How can I get the other person to do something that I want to do?" As a seductress, you have to think about how you can motivate your partner to par-ticipate. For example, if you want to go see a sappy movie and you know it's not the kind of film your partner likes, you have to get creative and think about how you can get her to come anyway. You promise popcorn and rave about the actress. You think about what she might go for. If you know her soft spots, you exploit them. Translated to the bedroom, this means: "How can I make sex appealing to my partner again?"

We've known each other so long. Wouldn't it be strange to suddenly pretend I don't know what my partner wants?

Rethink your understanding of seduction. In your daily life you're often trying to make what you want appealing to your partner. Why shouldn't you do the same with sex? Think about how you seduce him in other parts of life, and transfer this to sex. Let go of clichés. Seduction doesn't necessarily mean a garter belt and negligee. It starts long before sex. It could be text messages, long looks, playing with closeness and distance, casually stroking his arm and then going away again. But if you want to wear a garter belt: go for it! Courage always pays off.

In a long-term relationship, you experience a lot together and know each other inside and out. This is wonderful, but it also brings you so close that you rarely have a chance to long for your partner or see him from a distance. This happens automatically: the other person is always there. An erotic relationship therefore requires a little distance and space now and then: alone time. This is very important for your sexuality as well. I advise my patients to spend time alone or with friends, and to deliberately plan time for themselves. This leads to being excited about each other again—and maybe even to feeling in love.

Are there positions that can make it easier for me to come?

Yes and no. On the one hand, it depends on which parts of your vagina and vulva are best sensitized and connected to sexual response in your brain. If, for example, you've sensitized the G-zone, you'll reach orgasm more easily in positions that stimulate it. On the other hand, it's also a matter of the shape of your partner's penis. Generally, if you've discovered and sensitized all the areas of your vagina well, position is of secondary importance.

When I've done all ten steps, am I done with practicing, or do I have to do it all again after a while?

The connection between vagina and brain will get weaker if you stop spending time on your sex parts. But in principle, it's like playing the piano: you may get out of practice, but once you've reached a certain level, it's only a matter of brushing up your skills before you can play the pieces you once mastered. But apart from that: Why would you stop focusing on your sexuality, if it feels good?

Clara and Tom

CLARA IS FORTY-TWO. She's a mother of two and works in marketing. She came to see me because she wanted to get to know her body better, to rekindle her libido, and to come to orgasm "more easily." There were often long periods of time when she didn't feel any desire for sex, which her husband, Tom, turned into an accusation: it was her fault that their sex life wasn't great. At first, she thought he was right. She wanted to have more desire and "take care of the problem"—ultimately, she didn't want it to put a strain on their marriage. And so Clara came to therapy with me for several weeks, and Tom was very supportive. He encouraged her to engage with her sexuality: he wanted her to understand why he thinks sex is so wonderful.

Clara learned the exercises in this book, got to know her body better, and started to move more to increase her arousal. When she tried to put what she'd learned into practice with Tom, however, he was suddenly less enthusiastic. Clara wanted him to move more slowly and use his whole body instead of just his pelvis. Tom tried hard: he wanted to do everything right, especially since he was the one who encouraged Clara to go to therapy in the first place. But the implementation wasn't so easy. The tempo was a problem for him. When he moved more slowly, he got stressed. He was afraid of losing his erection, but he didn't say so. He just expressed his frustration that this kind of sex was so complicated. In addition, he had the feeling he was having sex according to a plan, and no longer according to his impulses. It goes against the spontaneity principle, he complained.

It's not rare for sex therapy to cause strain on a relationship for a while. I always tell my patients at the beginning that therapy can trigger uncertainty and anger. It's often easier to sweep certain things under the rug than to examine them more closely. When one person changes and then demands that the sex with their partner change too, it can shake up a lot of things.

I advise Clara to bring Tom with her. He agrees, and they come to see me together. In conversation I find out that Tom wishes Clara would just focus on him more often. He'd like to have long, intense blow-jobs, but Clara is often "too lazy." Clara says the same of her husband: Tom is "too lazy" to really take care of her needs—he's usually just interested in his own satisfaction.

They also both complain that they hardly have any time for each other. Their kids require a lot of time and attention, and they spend a lot of time out with friends. They notice that they haven't really been talking to each other for years. They do share things and talk about their daily lives, but just chatting or talking about their feelings or problems almost never happens. Nor do they spend evenings alone as a couple. If they're not with their kids, they're meeting friends. It's just usually more interesting, they say, though they both find this kind of sad.

In therapy they first learn to make changes on the emotional level, in their communication. They have to be more honest with each other, even when that can make things uncomfortable. They start by questioning the patterns that have become automatic in their relationship. Clara, for example, is always annoyed when Tom puts the dishes away "wrong, as usual." Tom says she shouldn't make such a fuss—he doesn't notice it, and he's certainly not intentionally doing it wrong. It's useful to take a closer look at such situations. Here too, they both need to learn to be more honest instead of just rolling their eyes in annoyance. Such conflicts can be defused if they're addressed in a direct, friendly way. Clara should explain clearly what she's annoyed about: that Tom is ignoring something that's important to her. She should tell him this—even if he doesn't want to hear it.

For good communication, it's important for couples not to hide behind platitudes. Certain patterns creep into many long-term relationships: in this case, one partner became resigned to the fact that the other "just doesn't want as much sex." That's frustrating, but also comfortable. Tom does complain sometimes, but since he's often stressed and exhausted himself, it's actually often fine with him that she's not asking him for sex on top of it.

Clara and Tom have to start speaking plainly to each other about sex as well. In conversation it becomes clear that in Tom's stressful everyday life, sex isn't really that important to him anymore, but it's easier for him to blame Clara for the lack of eroticism in their relationship. He didn't actually want to engage with the subject; he just wanted "everything to work well." It seemed like a perfect solution to him for his wife to see a sex therapist.

Clara and Tom realize as they're speaking with me that their marriage isn't working perfectly on other levels either. After his initial frustration, Tom realizes that he has to work on himself if he wants his marriage and sex life to improve. He starts coming to see me on his own.

Clara also continues coming to therapy with me. She has to learn not to suffer in silence but rather to express painful things, even if this leads to awkwardness in the short term. She also realizes that she's often annoyed because she expects to be annoyed in certain situations.

Both have realized that they have to actively make changes if they want things to change in their relationship. That might sound obvious at first, but it's not clear to many couples. Clara and Tom recognize that they have to make time for each other if they really want to be closer.

So they set aside weekends and evenings to spend alone as a couple. They plan sex into their daily lives and talk in therapy about what exactly they really want. Both had "kind of a sense," but they only understood each other's concrete, specific wishes when they started to talk about it. At first, they both found expressing these wishes uncomfortable because they were afraid their partner wouldn't be able to understand them. Getting over this took a while—which is perfectly normal. Ultimately, they both had to get used to their new openness toward each other.

We do various exercises together in therapy. For example, I ask Tom and Clara to touch each other first so that the person being touched enjoys it, then so that the toucher enjoys it. This helps them to break their patterns and try out new ways of touching each other—sometimes gentle, sometimes more intense, sometimes hard—and to notice how the different ways feel to each of them.

Clara and Tom's sex life gets better and better over time. Of course there are still phases when they have less sex, but there are no more long dry spells. When they haven't had sex for a while, it no longer takes as much effort to get back to it. They've both learned to say when they don't feel like having sex—but also when one or the other of them does feel like it. And they make sure that there's enough time for the two of them in their calendars.

AN OVERVIEW OF
THE EXERCISES

T o MAKE IT easier, here are the exercises from all ten steps laid out together.

STEP 1

Mini Anatomy Lesson:
The Vagina, Vulva, and Clitoris

1. Touch your vulva and vagina several times a week. How? Let's try a warm-up exercise. Make a loose fist with your left hand to symbolize your sex parts. Slowly insert your right index finger: What do you feel? Where is it soft? Where is it warm? Are there rough spots? How this makes your fist (or your vagina) feel is unimportant— the focus should be on what your finger touches. Ultimately, the idea is to discover what your vulva and vagina feel like. Try to smile while you're doing the

exercise—this will trigger positive emotions in your brain, which will in turn make the exercise easier.

2. Think as precisely as possible about how you feel arousal. Where do you feel it? What does it feel like? Do you really physically feel something, or does it happen more on an emotional level? Many women find it hard to describe their arousal in words and sometimes don't even notice when they're aroused, even though their bodies show signs of it. Try to pay close attention to the tiny changes that happen to your sex parts.

STEP 2
Where Do I Stand?
My Body and What I Like

1. Observe yourself during masturbation and answer the questionnaire on page 33. Do everything just as you usually do it. If you've never, or only rarely, masturbated, start now and let intuition be your guide. Just do what feels good. Masturbation can be any way you pleasure yourself without a partner—by touching yourself in various ways, using a vibrator, squeezing your legs together, etc. The goal of this exercise is to end up with as precise a description as possible—a kind of masturbation log. Masturbate several times a week: observing yourself might distract you and muddle your normal routine, so it might take some time to get an accurate picture.

2. Figure out how you feel about your sex parts. How do you include them in your daily life? How aware are you of your vagina and vulva? When do you think about them? And when you do think about them, are your thoughts positive or negative? Send your sex parts a mental text now and then to ask how they're doing.

STEP 3

Where Do I Come From?
My Sexual Past

FROM NOW ON you'll begin slowly expanding on your usual patterns. You might want to try suddenly changing everything at once, but that won't work. As so often in life, you need a bit of time and patience.

Change one detail when you masturbate and observe how it feels. If you usually move your fingers fairly quickly, or use a lot of pressure, try to go slowly and more gently. Or try to change the amount of tension in your body or to vary the tempo.

When you notice that you're no longer feeling much and your arousal is diminishing, return to your trusty old ways. Let your arousal grow, and then start again with the new version, the changed rhythms. It's important to not suddenly change your whole technique, but rather change just one element of it. Otherwise you might completely lose your arousal. Repeat the exercise several times a week. It doesn't matter whether you ultimately come this way or not.

STEP 4

Move It!
Why Movement Matters

1. Start moving when you masturbate. Circle your hips. Swing back and forth. Try to not just lie there. Consciously tense your muscles and then relax them. When your arousal diminishes—as it probably will—return to your reliable pattern and use it to increase your arousal. Then start moving again—only a little at first. With time you'll notice that your arousal lasts longer and you feel more and more. If you don't come to orgasm, it's okay. Repeat this exercise several times a week.

2. Touch your vagina inch by inch, and consciously observe how it feels in different places. Create an internal map of your vagina. How does it feel right at the front? How about an inch farther in on the left side? What does the G-zone feel like?

    Try to be more conscious of your vagina throughout the day. You've touched your vulva and vagina many times now; you know how they feel and how they're built. Try to work your sex parts into your daily life. Walk so that you feel your vagina. Repeatedly tense and release the muscles of your pelvic floor. Breathe deep into your abdomen. Try to consciously perceive your vagina. And—even more important!—try to develop a sense of pride in it.

3. Imagine there's a clock face at the entrance to your vagina. Determine where 12, 3, 6, and 9 o'clock are. Now touch the entrance to your vagina with one or two fingers. How do these specific spots feel? Now imagine the clock face is deeper in your vagina. Touch the four spots again, now farther inside. How does each of these spots feel? Do you feel differences? Where are you sensitive, where less sensitive?

   This is a good exercise to involve your partner in: How precisely do you feel which spot he's touching? What changes when he touches different spots? And what difference does it make when it's not your finger that you feel, but his?

STEP 5
The Pelvic Floor: Why It's So Important

1. Sit on a chair with your back straight and your feet on the floor. Tense the muscles of your pelvic floor as if you're trying to stop yourself from peeing. Now imagine your pelvic floor is an elevator: tense the muscles going up and down, concentrating on the "descent." Try to really let go at the end—it should feel as if you're about to pee your pants.

2. Several times a day, tense the muscles of your pelvic floor for three seconds, and then slowly release them. After the intense contraction, the relaxation will be

deeper. This is therefore a reliable way to get your pelvic muscles to relax.

3. Practice breathing into your belly. Place your hand on your belly and wait until it curves when you breathe in. Now try to breathe more deeply with each breath. Let your belly grow big like a balloon, then let it contract, and blow it up again.

4. Put your hand on your vulva and try to feel your breathing there. What do your fingers feel when you breathe in and out deeply?

5. If you're already easily able to tense and release the muscles of your pelvic floor, you can try playing with the individual muscles. Tense first your left butt cheek, then your right. Now tense the muscles around your anus, and then the muscles farther forward, by your vagina and urethra. Then try to release the muscles of your anus while keeping the front ones tensed. You'll never be able to completely separately control these muscles, because they're complexly intertwined. But the better you learn to control them, the more specifically they can transport your arousal.

STEP 6

All in Your Head?
Sexual Fantasies

1. Start to write down your sexual fantasies and notice whether they change over time. When you change the way you stimulate yourself, your fantasies will also change. If you find writing down your fantasies uncomfortable, just note down keywords. If that's hard too, observe yourself the next time you masturbate. What are you thinking about, what arouses you, what do you think about right before orgasm? Do you enjoy your fantasies or are you ashamed of them? A few weeks later, observe yourself again. Has anything changed in your mental movie?

2. Change another detail when you masturbate and notice how it feels. Instead of changing your rhythm or pressure, for example, change your position. If you usually lie on your back, turn over onto your stomach. Or stand. Or sit. If your arousal subsides, return to your usual position. Repeat the exercise several times a week.

STEP 7

Swing It!
The Pelvic Swing

1. Practice the pelvic swing on its own—not while masturbating or having sex. It's not about arousal at this point, but rather about getting your body to understand and internalize the movement so that you don't have to concentrate on it anymore. If you lie on your back to masturbate, work the pelvic swing into your routine in this position first. Try to steer the motion from your back, and not with your legs or the muscles of your buttocks. During the exercise, imagine picking something up and drawing it in with the vagina, and then letting it go. When the movement functions well in this position, go on to the next position and practice it that way at least four times. Practice the seated pelvic swing whenever you're sitting and waiting somewhere. Repeat the pelvic swing in various positions so often that you no longer have to think about it, and your body makes the motion automatically. But be careful—don't try to do everything at once. Every time you practice, just concentrate on one of the four positions.

2. Put your finger in the entrance to the vagina and see if you feel the desire to take it farther inside. You can move your finger, or just keep it still inside you. If you want to practice with arousal and you find it subsiding,

arouse yourself as you usually do. If you're lying on your back and feel like your arm isn't long enough, put a pillow under your pelvis, or lie on your stomach and curl your legs up underneath you like a ball.

STEP 8

Be More Self-Centered! Pay Attention to You

1. Place one or more fingers on your vulva. If you like, get it wet first with saliva, lube, or oil. Instead of moving your fingers, move your pelvis. Swing and make circles. Think of a cat that wants to be petted—you just have to hold your hand out and it will rub up against it where it wants to be touched. Do it like a cat, holding your hand still and getting the stimulation you want by moving your body. Notice what you feel, and whether it feels different than when you lie still. You can also place one or more fingers in your vagina. Just keep your hand still, and use the pelvic swing to make your fingers slide in and out. Practice this several times a week.

2. Practice being selfish! When you're having sex, try to be conscious of what feels good and what doesn't. When your attention wanders to your partner, direct it back toward yourself. And even more important: move more during sex, so that you get what feels good to you.

STEP 9

Swing It Together!
Movement in Duet

1. Integrate movement into sex. If it gets too complicated and you're too in your head, concentrate more on your sensations and try not to think too much about perfect execution of the pelvic swing. The most important thing is that you feel more.

2. Start moving your upper body when you masturbate, and start using your voice and making your breath audible. Notice how this changes your experience.

STEP 10

Blasting Off Together:
A Lifetime of Good Sex

1. This exercise was invented by the systemic sex therapist Ulrich Clement, and I like to use it with my patients. The abbreviated version can work like this: You and your partner write down your sexual wishes, or even a whole ideal sexual scenario on a piece of paper and put what you've written in separate envelopes. In the next step, talk about whether you want to open the other person's envelope, and what doing so would mean. You don't have to open them, and if you do, you don't have to put them into practice—that's not the main point. Rather, this should help you figure

out what you want together, and how you feel about your partner's sexual desires. Do you really want to know about them? Are you really interested in them in the long term?

2. Use the party principle. When you hear critical voices in your head telling you you're not allowed to be a sex-craving being, take active notice of them and decide whether you want to give them space. If you don't want to give them space, give *yourself* space: move as much as possible, even if you don't really feel like it. Take initiative! Be twice as active! Be particularly passionate! Imagine you're in the middle of the dance floor having the time of your life, even if you originally wanted to stay home on the couch.

AND NOW,
HAVE FUN!

THE ESSENTIAL MESSAGE of the ten steps is as simple as it is challenging: good sex is a matter of practice— as is the orgasm you experience with it. The more you're grounded in your body, the better you know it and the more you feel, the less your desire and arousability will be dependent on external factors. Gradually, sex can become a resource that can help you to relax, or to create closeness with your partner. The small, unstable sapling in the first image will become, through good care (meaning practice), a tall, well-rooted tree that has nothing to fear from even the strongest gust of wind.

SEXUAL DESIRES

ILLNESSES
STRESS

FAMILY PROBLEMS

SEXUAL AROUSABILITY

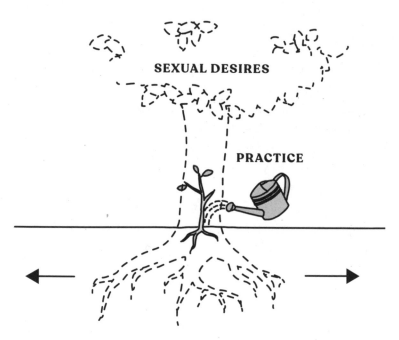

SEXUAL DESIRES

PRACTICE

SEXUAL AROUSABILITY

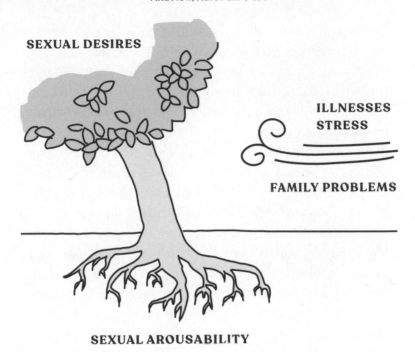

SEXUAL DESIRES

ILLNESSES
STRESS

FAMILY PROBLEMS

SEXUAL AROUSABILITY

THE PATH WILL look a bit different for every woman, as every woman learns differently and starts from a different place. This book offers support and inspiration for you to have a new experience of your own sexuality and desire. Your development probably won't be linear. Some exercises may be very easy for you, while others you may find difficult. You may immediately feel more, but not have an orgasm. Or the other way around: you might be surprised by an orgasm during sex with your partner, even though according to the plan, you still have steps to complete. There's no hard-and-fast rule for how sex works and what a woman has to do to come to orgasm. We all perceive touch differently and find different things arousing.

It's also possible that you'll intellectually understand all the exercises and suggestions in this book, but that you'll have a hard time grasping them physically and putting them into practice. Don't put pressure on yourself and don't worry—if this is the case for you, it can really help to find a good sex therapist in your area.

In any case, there's never a single goal that you can achieve once and for all. You'll never discover the perfect sex and be able to keep it that way forever. It's like playing piano. At some point you know a lot of pieces by heart, but you're excited to learn more, because it's relatively easy for you to do so. And with sex, there's an extra person involved. The way the sex turns out is therefore heavily dependent on your partner. But what your body feels as arousing and how much you enjoy the sex is under your control. This book should help you to get the maximum out of the sex you have, regardless of who you have it with—because you'll be able to become aroused in many different ways.

Life isn't linear. There will be times in life when sex isn't so important to you. That's fine! Don't drive yourself crazy if there are times when you just don't feel like engaging with your body and your sexuality. Be patient with yourself. But allow yourself to be curious! The great thing about sex is that the more intensively we engage with it, the more fascinating and exciting it becomes. Sex is a lifelong discovery! Have fun with it.

OF INTEREST
FOR AND ABOUT MEN

WOMEN AREN'T THE only ones who struggle with problems of desire and orgasm. For men too—contrary to all preconceptions—reaching and enjoying climax during sex with a partner can be a big challenge.

Some men feel too little when they have sex with a condom. Others blame the changes to their partners' bodies after childbirth for their own trouble reaching orgasm during sex. Still others think their age is responsible for their dwindling desire, or perhaps their appetite and arousal have never worked the way they imagined they ought to. Some men worry they won't be able to please their partners, which has a negative effect on their ability to come. Some come too quickly, others feel they take too long. Still others are so overwhelmed by the presence of their partners that they barely notice their own sensations.

Since sex doesn't always work perfectly easily, some men prefer masturbation, because unlike during sex with a partner, the man can concentrate fully on himself.

But when sex with a partner doesn't always work easily, it's not because there's anything wrong with her vagina. Nor does desire simply diminish over time. It's also not the fault of age when a man's erections aren't as reliable and hard as they were at the beginning of the relationship. The cause is actually primarily the power of habit. Men too have particular techniques, use particular fantasies, and follow a particular pattern when they want to come to orgasm. If a man wants to improve his sex life, the same goes for him as goes for a woman: he has to develop his repertoire and discover new sources of arousal, sensitize the nerve endings in his penis, and strengthen the pathways to the brain, creating more synaptic connections.

Some men always rub back and forth in the same way when they masturbate. They only use one "information superhighway" between the penis and brain in order to come to orgasm. In addition, one's own hand is always much tighter and rougher than a vagina could ever be.

The penis must therefore be trained, just like the vagina. It contains various sensors and different erogenous zones, and, when sensitized, is well capable of perceiving the subtle stimulation of a vagina. If only the sensors that react to a man's hand are activated, the others are still undeveloped. In order to be more sensitive to the gentler feeling of a vagina, a man can train by using less pressure from his hand—making the hand more and more vagina-like. Then it won't matter how his partner's vagina is shaped, or if there's a condom between penis and vagina.

Good to know

How can a man sensitize his penis and thereby broaden his repertoire?

Another whole book could be written on the subject. In brief, for the man, too, the path to increased sensitivity is through masturbation. The best way to begin is by using lube—this is a way of practicing holding the erection even when the friction isn't as strong. If that goes well, he can stimulate his penis more slowly, reducing the tempo of his hand movements. If he's able to hold out for longer thanks to this change of pace, he can also try standing up while he masturbates. If this works, I recommend breathing more deeply and thereby relaxing more. Once this step has been mastered, the man can experiment with moving his penis by using his hips, instead of moving his hand. This is a way of learning to control his penis and his ejaculation. Instead of imitating masturbation when he has sex, he does it the other way around and imitates sex when he masturbates.

What should a man do if he likes to watch porn when he masturbates?

There's nothing wrong with porn per se. There's only a problem when the man always watches porn when he masturbates. If he's used to being bombarded by stimulation from the screen, he'll rely on that for his arousal. When a man has just fallen in love, at first the new woman is enough to cause sufficient arousal. But after several years, she lacks the allure that comes with newness. The stimulation he gets through his eyes is now too weak. Of course, this isn't the fault of the woman, but rather the fault of the man's lopsided arousal pattern: he hasn't learned to develop arousal from within himself. And that's precisely what it comes down to in sex with a partner. Arousal can be developed in ways other than through visual stimulation. For that to work, it's important for him use all of his erogenous zones.

Men too have many more erogenous zones than just the penis, and it's a lot of fun to discover them and incorporate them into sex.

More active sex with more motion and emotion: Tips for men

IF YOU'RE READING this, your partner has probably read this book, and she's sensitized her vagina and learned to move her whole body and particularly her pelvis more during sex. If you're also curious about how to develop your sex life, read this chapter.

Some women hold their bodies very tense during sex. And many men are also fairly stiff. They pound away like a jackhammer with tensed muscles, a rigid body, and great effort. This can lead to quick or premature ejaculation. Many men have this problem in the missionary position. In order to hold themselves up over their partner, they tense their muscles and keep their body fairly stiff. This tension increases their arousal very quickly so that they come without really being able to concentrate on what they're feeling, and despite the fact that they might actually want to have longer sex. But too much tension can lead to erection problems, because it keeps the penis from receiving enough blood flow. The familiar in-and-out might also stop working so well if your partner starts using the pelvic swing (described in Step 7), which absorbs your thrusts.

The same goes for you as for your partner: more pleasurable and intense sex requires movement, otherwise the muscles won't receive enough blood flow. And parts of the body that receive good blood flow are more sensitive and feel better than those that are tense. Yet some men are highly tense during sex and move their pelvis little. If you want to feel more and exploit the whole range of sexual options with your partner, you should practice movements that come from the hips—for example the pelvic swing. The pelvic swing doesn't just have advantages for the woman and for your sex together: rather, when you learn the movement, you can control your penis better, arouse yourself more, feel more, and decide when you want to come to orgasm. And your orgasm may feel much more intense than before.

Practice alone at first. If you relax and move your pelvis when you masturbate, you'll notice that you have a very different feeling than when you just rub or press with your hands. This has to do with the fact that the movement helps your pelvis receive more circulation, and so you perceive your arousal more. You can use the pelvic swing for sex in any position. Don't be surprised if it takes a while to feel the positive effects. It's even possible that you'll feel less at first.

The pelvic swing requires practice and a new way of thinking. Some men control their movements during sex primarily with the muscles of their buttocks, which leads to tension. The pelvic swing works differently: the back does the work, and the buttocks are less tight. A great side benefit: a man who uses his hips more and has sensitized his penis will feel it extending deep inside, and thus have the impression that his penis is larger and better looking.

PELVIC SWING EXERCISES FOR MEN

The pelvic swing while standing

THE PELVIC SWING is fairly difficult to execute while standing, since straight legs make a loose, easy motion difficult. In this position, the man is tensed like a bow and can't help moving fairly stiffly. Therefore, make sure that your knees are slightly bent—this is the only way the movement will be possible.

At first, try placing a chair against the wall and supporting your knees against it. This will help you keep your knees in the right position instead of straightening them.

The pelvic swing on all fours

TRY THE PELVIC swing on all fours—you should rest on your knees, with your hands shoulder-width apart. Now think of the way a cat arches its back. Assume this position and imagine your back is being pulled toward the ceiling. It may be helpful to exaggerate the movement a bit. Then move your back downward into a U-shape. Repeat this movement several times and try to make the motion slowly and fluidly. Breathe deep into your belly. When you arch your back, the air flows out, and when your stomach and back sink downward, your belly fills with air.

The pelvic swing on your back

FOR THIS VARIATION, you lie on your back with your legs bent. When you make the U-shape, your mid-back lifts off the bed or other surface, and when you arch your back, it presses down. The buttocks don't move but remain resting on the bed.

The pelvic swing in the missionary position

THE MISSIONARY POSITION poses a challenge, because you have to use your muscles to hold yourself up. This causes some men to get stiff and tense. This keeps them from being able to control their arousal, which may cause them to come too quickly.

You can practice the pelvic swing in the missionary position this way:

* Place two pillows on the ground. Lie on top of them as if they were your partner's torso. Imagine that your pelvis is on top of hers. Your knees are slightly bent, and

your lower legs can rest on the ground. Your weight is on your lower arms, your pelvis, and your lower legs.

* Now you do the pelvic swing. First you arch your back a bit—as if your mid-back is being pulled toward the ceiling. Then make a U-shape. Imagine as you do so that you're penetrating your partner's vagina: when you arch your back, your penis moves easily forward; in the U-shape, it moves back. The important thing is that your pelvis keeps moving.

The pelvic swing while masturbating

WHEN YOU USE your hand to masturbate, it probably does all the work and your body barely moves. If you use the pelvic swing, the opposite is the case: you use only your hips to move your penis into and out of your hand. You can try the movement in every position. Use lube or oil so that it slides well. This will make your masturbation as much like sex as it can be.

Arousal is a matter of practice

IF YOU LOSE your arousal when you practice, it's because this kind of arousal is entirely new to you. Changing arousal patterns is often difficult for men, because their erections can sometimes suffer. In addition, many men struggle with fear of failure.

Don't give up right away. You can always go back to your old technique now and then and see that it still works. Keep your eyes on the prize, step-by-step. Not because you want to be the perfect lover, but because you want to feel more and have a more wide-ranging, exciting sex life. You'll feel stronger when you discover more about your desire and sexuality.

FOR WOMEN WHO
LOVE WOMEN

WOMEN ARE ALWAYS confronted with basically similar issues when they want to explore their sexuality —regardless of sexual orientation and whether they sleep with women, men, or both.

My book is primarily directed toward women. Above all, it deals with the female body and women's sexuality—men play a supporting role and are mentioned only peripherally. My core message is: *Dear women, get to know your bodies and your sex parts and you will enjoy sex more.* This book focuses on the vagina, but with the knowledge that female sexuality is a much, much broader topic. The better you know your own sexuality, the more you'll want to be touched. By sensitizing your vagina, you can give yourself a new source of sensitivity and arousal—but this is optional. Most women are already familiar with the sensitivities and sensations of their clitoris, so this is only mentioned at the beginning of the book. You may be satisfied and happy with what you already know—and that's perfectly fine! As I said before: the vagina is an additional area that can be developed if you so choose. Sex certainly doesn't have to involve vaginal penetration if you don't enjoy it, but the choice is up to you.

There are still many stereotypes about lesbian sexuality and sex between women, and too little research—particularly in comparison to studies of heterosexual couples. There have been several studies of lesbian sexuality, but since they focused on different issues, their results were contradictory.

Take, for example, studies that seek to determine frequency of sex. They always focus on the kind of sex where a penis penetrates a vagina. These studies say nothing about the duration of the act, about foreplay, intensity, creativity, or anything else. Yet the latter categories are the ones we usually use to evaluate sexual fulfillment. Measured against such studies, female couples have sex less frequently, but their sex is often longer, more intense, more passionate, erotic, and creative, and doesn't focus solely on the sex parts, but includes other erogenous zones.

Every woman therefore faces the same tasks when she wants to learn about her body, regardless of her sexual orientation. It can't be said enough: sex isn't penetration, sex isn't intercourse, sex includes an endless range of ways to play with the whole body and with arousal. Sex comprises infinite variety, and this book seeks to illuminate only one specific aspect.

Exercises

THE GOAL OF the following exercises is to perceive the fine differences between a finger or fingers and a dildo, and to train your vagina. They are aimed toward women in relationships with other women, but could also be interesting for heterosexual women and couples!

1. Take a dildo and insert it slowly into your vagina. Try to pause and sense precisely what it feels like. How are you holding it in your hand? How do you move it? Where? And how does it feel when you change your hand position, turning it more to the right or left than usual? Then: Where do you feel arousal? Do you really feel something in your body, or is it more mental? Try to sense precisely how your sex parts are affected in even the slightest ways. If you repeat this exercise, the dildo will start to feel more and more like an extension of your hand and less like a sterile tool. You'll develop a feeling for what happens at the front end of the dildo. This will help you show your partner what exactly you like and where she should touch you with her fingers or the dildo.

2. Insert a finger into your partner's vagina. Consider where exactly your attention is—is it really on your finger and what your finger is doing? Are you trying to sense what your finger is doing? What do you perceive? Do you enjoy what you're doing with your finger, or are you just executing an action? Think about what arouses you when you arouse your partner. Is it

her arousal? Perhaps your attention is solely on her, and you look at her face to see if she likes what you're doing. Or are you able to actually enjoy penetrating her with your finger? Do you get pleasure from penetrating her, from actively entering another body?

Switch fingers and notice how it feels with the fingers of the right hand compared with the fingers of the left. Consider what different spots you can reach with different fingers, and how this changes your sensations.

Good to know

How is the advice in this book different for women who have sex with women?

It's no different than the advice about heterosexual sex. The crux is the development of one's own sex parts, regardless of sexual orientation. Lesbian women have similar challenges in relationships as heterosexual women, bisexual women, polyamorous women, and so on. The task is always the same: to connect with your own body and sexuality. To discover their full potential, to develop them, and to make many different sensations available to them.

Do female couples need a substitute for a penis to get the most out the steps in this book?

Not at all! Every couple has infinite possibilities to play with and discover. It's nice for lesbian couples to experiment with fingers or the mouth in different positions, and to try out all kinds of stimulation and penetration. Different fingers and objects will reach different spots. You can also experiment with different kinds and sizes of dildos or strap-ons, if you want to.

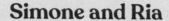

Simone and Ria

SIMONE AND RIA ARE both in their late thirties when they come to me. They've been happily together for a long time, though the beginning of their relationship was somewhat rocky. Simone grew up in a family where homosexuality wasn't spoken of openly. Her parents always kept a close watch on her, which greatly shaped her development—in particular her relationship with her own body and sexuality. Simone always wore clothing that wasn't "typically feminine," but her parents kept buying her frilly pink things. She was constantly accused of being "half boy." Her parents gave her Barbies, though she had no interest in them. They were driven by their own needs to squeeze their daughter into a stereotypical feminine role.

The fact that Simone wasn't supported in her interests and in her development, but instead was always made to feel wrong and insufficient, shaped her life significantly. Her conservative parents frequently told her that she had a choice, and that it would be easier for those around her if she were to live in a heterosexual relationship.

Ria, on the other hand, had liberal parents who were very open to homosexuality. At the same time, she could tell that her parents would have been happier if she were heterosexual. And so she had to hear comments like "Maybe the right guy just hasn't come along yet!" or "Maybe you'll still find a man who suits you!" Even though her sexuality was basically accepted, she still had to suffer the question of whether there wasn't perhaps a way to change it.

These kinds of comments have a huge impact. Simone and Ria always had to actively position themselves to deal with their environments, which made free sexual development more difficult. In therapy, we worked through particular sites of trauma so that they could leave these burdens behind them. The goal was to enable them, for example, to make out in public if they felt like it, without having to look over their shoulders. Yet they still get comments when they kiss or hold hands on the street, and sometimes have to struggle with open hostility.

In therapy, Simone and Ria expressed the desire to make their sex life more interesting again. They had both essentially developed a healthy sexuality, but found that the things that worked best were usually the things they were most familiar with. For example, as soon as they brought a sex toy into play, things got trickier.

Together, they had already discovered and explored clitoral sex and sex with their fingers. Over the years, they've opened up to each other and have gotten comfortable showing each other what they like. They've explored each other's bodies and have found lots of ways to play. Their vaginas, however, were never a big part of their sex lives. This, of course, is perfectly fine, and Simone and Ria did not need their sex to involve penetration if they were happy with what they were doing. At some point, though, they decided they would like to experiment with the vagina and discover more. But it's not quite working perfectly yet.

The problem with vaginal stimulation is that they feel too little when they use dildos or strap-ons, and that goes for both the person being penetrated and the penetrator. It therefore isn't much fun, and even hurts sometimes.

We talk about the fact that it's totally normal for vaginal stimulation not to be super arousing at first. The vagina has a lot of untapped potential that has to be discovered and developed. This potential will simply sleep peacefully if it isn't awoken. And so I suggest that they try the two exercises above—each of them on their own. The point of the first exercise is to make how the dildo is used by the other person less important for the person being penetrated, because once she learns where her points of arousal are, she can move her body and position her erogenous zones the way she needs to.

The penetrating partner has a different mission: How can she sense what the dildo or strap-on touches? It's the same task as the one that faces an apprentice cook holding a knife for the first time. Or a surgeon, assisting at her first procedure. Both have to learn to know their tools so well and sharpen their perception so keenly that they can "feel" what's happening in the tip of their knife or scalpel.

A woman who wants to penetrate her girlfriend with a dildo can learn to connect her sensations to the dildo so closely that it will ultimately start to work like an extension of her hand. She can do this by immersing herself and paying more and more attention to the movements she makes. Her movements should be very deliberate and at times very slow. Only through slow, deliberate movements can she learn to better sense what she's touching. Once she's really developed her feel for the dildo over time, she can start to speed it up. And, of course, if the couple preferred not to use a dildo, they could use their fingers or hands instead.

THEORY FOR THE
KNOWLEDGE SEEKER:
THE FOUR TYPES
OF AROUSAL

Y APPROACH AS a sex therapist, on which my daily work with patients and this book is based, comes largely from Jean-Yves Desjardins's concept of the "sexocorporel." Desjardins was a Canadian psychologist and professor of clinical sexology who developed the concept through years of research. The sexocorporel approach offers a comprehensive and precise description of sexual phenomena which allows, when necessary, a specific diagnosis and a treatment tailored to it. (You can find more information on this approach, available in English, German, French, and Italian, at sexocorporel.com.) Sex therapy based on Jean-Yves Desjardins's findings aims to quickly and effectively fulfill the needs of women, men, and couples who want to experience more from their sex-uality and in their relationships.

In order to change the quality of my patients' sex lives through learnable steps, I first try to find out in con-versation how their sexuality functions and what their strengths and limitations are. According to the sexocor-porel theory, the various patterns of arousal can be divided into four basic types.

Remember Step 2, where you surveyed your arousal— how you arouse yourself, how you increase your arousal, and how you trigger the orgasm reflex alone or with a partner? Some patients find it very interesting to learn more about these types in order to recognize which mode they primarily use to arouse themselves. Most people use some combination of the modes that Desjardins described. Each of these modes has strengths and limitations. Some of them work better for long, indulgent sex and orgasms triggered through the vagina, while others are more suited to a quickie or masturbation.

In trying to place yourself in one of the four types, it may be your goal to discover which of the modes you've used most often to arouse yourself in the past. This will make it easier for you to expand your arousability to include the other options, so that, ultimately, you'll be able to experience sexual pleasure in as many different ways as possible. Let's take a closer look at the four modes.

Archaic mode

PEOPLE WHO PRIMARILY stimulate themselves in this mode elicit arousal mainly through pressure and tension. Even babies experience a pleasant feeling when they press their legs together. Some people stick to this pressure method throughout their lives and use it to come to orgasm. Women particularly tend to use this mode: one third of women, to be precise. In this mode, women sit or lie on their stomachs with their legs crossed. Little motion is necessary; instead, the woman exerts pressure on her sex parts by pressing her legs together, or with the muscles of the pelvic floor. The great advantage of this is that it works anywhere, even in the subway. But a woman who's used to pressing her legs together to arouse herself may lose this arousal as soon as she spreads her legs, which can lead to challenges in sex with a partner. This way of increasing arousal is very targeted and efficient. It's not well-suited to long, indulgent sessions.

Those who arouse themselves in the archaic mode:

* like pressure,
* move little,
* tense their bodies,
* usually press their legs together, and
* breathe shallowly.

Mechanical mode

ANOTHER KIND OF sexual arousal involves mechanically rubbing the genitals. More men use this mode than women. It's characterized by quick, automatic motions. Men rub their penises, come, and that's it. Women make rubbing motions or hold a vibrator on their clitoris to come to orgasm. In this mode, too, little is moved other than the hand. The mechanical mode is the most common: forty to sixty percent of all people increase their arousal and bring themselves to orgasm this way.

This mode usually works very well alone, and can also be integrated well into partner sex. Still, it can run into problems if either the spot that needs to be rubbed or stroked or the manner of the touch is very specific. If the partner uses a different technique, it can be difficult for people of this type. If the partner doesn't stimulate us exactly the way we're used to, the arousal ebbs away. Many women of this type are used to using a vibrator to come. A vibrator's high frequency can't be replicated by a hand or tongue or penis.

The same goes for the man. If the penis is used to the strong pressure of his own hand, his partner's mouth or vagina may be too weak. If a man is used to rubbing very quickly when he masturbates, he may have problems with sex because he can't thrust as quickly as is necessary for his arousal.

Arousal through partner sex can be a significant challenge for people of this type, because the stimulation of sex feels very different from the arousal pattern they learned alone. Since women of this type primarily rub their clitoris and labia, they often don't find penetrative sex—what happens in the vagina, that is—very arousing.

Those who arouse themselves in the mechanical mode:
* like friction and vibration,
* move little,
* tense their bodies,
* breathe shallowly,
* are easily distracted, and
* stimulate their external sex parts.

Undulatory mode

THE UNDULATORY MODE makes use of broad, supple, fluid movements. The body moves in all directions during sex, the breath is deep, and the muscles relaxed. This mode is playful and sensual, and arousal is experienced as very pleasurable. Men rarely belong to this type. The more a person moves in this mode, the more erogenous zones they develop. The arousal is distributed through the whole body and is experienced very strongly. In the undulatory mode, people can often completely surrender themselves to their arousal.

Women can enjoy this mode indefinitely—sometimes for hours, even. They love being connected to their partner and to themselves. But they often can't increase their arousal to the point of orgasm. They can't channel themselves to a climax. This can be frustrating, since they don't reach the goal, and at some point, the arousal dissipates. Some people therefore switch into one of the first two modes to bring themselves over the edge.

Those who arouse themselves in the undulatory mode:
* like being touched all over their bodies,
* move a lot and in all directions,
* are relaxed,
* breathe deeply,
* become immersed in their arousal, and
* have difficulty reaching orgasm.

Wave mode

PEOPLE WHO BELONG to this type use the whole field of sensual experience. They alternate during sex between focused movements and loose, easygoing ones. They play with muscle tension, movement, tempo, and space. The arousal can flow through the whole body.

In this mode, all possibilities for pleasure are open. People of this type can be aroused in extremely varied ways, which makes them less prone to distraction and disturbance. Women and men in this mode are able to submerge themselves in the game of lovemaking and tune out the world around them. Arousal usually works unproblematically for them and without great effort. Those who arouse themselves in wave mode increase their arousal to the point of orgasm through rhythmic movements of the pelvis. This creates the perfect mixture of dispersal and channeling of the arousal in the upper and lower body.

Those who have mastered this mode can control when and how they come to orgasm, and can get the maximum enjoyment out of it.

The wave mode provides the best conditions for an orgasm through penetrative sex. This book shows you step-by-step how you can arouse yourself and enjoy sex this way.

Those who arouse themselves in the wave mode:

* move rhythmically,
* have mastered the pelvic swing,
* like being touched all over their bodies,
* alternately tense and relax their bodies,
* breathe deeply,
* become immersed in their arousal, and
* can have an orgasm through vaginal stimulation.

ACKNOWLEDGMENTS

FOR FOURTEEN YEARS I have worked professionally, academically, and therapeutically on the topic of sexuality. There have always been voices who wanted to hold me back, who told me I should do something more sensible. For me, there was nothing more sensible than supporting others' exploration of their sexuality—for sex is so much more than the word is usually taken to mean. It's as much a part of being human as eating and breathing. Sexuality has endless aspects and can be expressed in infinite ways. I am very grateful to be able to follow my dream, remain true to my passion, and continue to explore step-by-step. This book is a further contribution to this goal, and a way of sharing my experiences.

Thank you from the bottom of my heart to my husband and children for your tireless support and love, and for the time you spend with me. I learn a great deal from and with you!

Many thanks go to Annette Bischof-Campbell for her friendship, her professional support, and for our work

together with the group "Toward orgasm, with pleasure."
She is executive director of the sex education website
lilli.info, so I have her to thank for that website's incredibly
valuable texts and information, which provided inspiration and models for my book. I'm very glad to be a member
of the Lilli team myself. You can find more information
about Lilli in the next section.

Thank you to all the teachers who have helped me along
this path, supported me, and encouraged me to keep
learning, including Peter Gehrig, Karoline Bischof, Ulrich
Clement, Jakob Pastötter, and David Schnarch. I look forward to many more years of learning and development.
Many thanks also to Ann-Marlene Henning, who supported me in word and deed as this book was coming to be.

Thank you to my friends and family, who like me
despite all my craziness.

And thank you of course to all my patients*: for the
privilege of supporting them through a part of their lives
and for always challenging me.

Last but not least, thank you to Nicole Kim for her
drawings, and to my editor Anja Hänsel, who was always
patient with me. I also offer my deepest thanks for help
with the writing.

*Patient comes, by the way, from the Latin patio, which means patience ☺.

What is lilli.info?

LILLI.INFO IS A website is aimed at young adults, with the goal of preventing violence and promoting sexual health. The online offerings are accessible, free, and anonymous. Without providing an email address, users can ask questions and have them answered by doctors, psychologists, psychotherapists, sex therapists, and sex counselors. The content of all online advice from the last three years is available to all users, as are over four hundred articles with tips and information.

Lilli.info was founded in 2001 and is more popular than ever. The site now receives over ten thousand visitors per day. What was originally a small site addressing date rape has grown to a comprehensive online source of information about sexuality, contraception, violence, relationships, and male- and female-specific topics without which the landscape of counseling in Switzerland has become unimaginable.

As a resource about sexual health and violence, Lilli makes professional knowledge available to service providers in related fields; the site has partnerships with and membership in various related organizations. Through networking, Lilli aims to provide young people with access to the best and most current help and information available.

Lilli is an independent, tax-exempt non-profit financed through donations from foundations, states, municipalities, congregations, and individuals.

APPENDIX

Helpful links and contacts

daniaschiftan.ch
lilli.info
sexocorporel.com

For an intimate portrait of modern sex, sexuality, and love, I recommend the book *Let's Talk About Sex: Real Stories From a Therapists Office* by my colleague and renowned sexologist Ann-Marlene Henning (Greystone Books, 2020).

INDEX

Note: Page numbers in italics refer to illustrations.

archaic mode of arousal,
183
arousal: four modes of,
183–87; patterns of,
32, 55, 58, 90, 111–12;
physical, 20, 35–38,
36, 37, 40, 120–21, 124;
sources of (*see* erotica;
pornography; sexual
fantasies)
arousal paradox, 74
arousal reflex, 68–69, 85,
121

Bischof-Campbell,
Annette, 2
breathing, 65, 76, 122–
24, 150

cerebral cortex, 29–31, *30*
cervix, 14, *14*, 15, 17, 22
childbirth, effects of,
77–78, 80, 161
childhood sexuality,
6–7, 50, 51–52, 54,
55, 57, 176
Clement, Ulrich, 135, 136,
154
clitoral orgasm, 8, 22–23,
50–51. *See also* orgasm
clitoris, 11, 12–13, *13*, 16.
See also crura; glans
condoms, 18, 161
crura ("legs" of clitoris),
12, *13, 14*, 21
curves of arousal, 20,
35–38, *36, 37*, 40,